—LOST LINES—
NORTH EASTERN

NIGEL WELBOURN

IAN ALLAN Publishing

C O N T E N T S

		Page
	Introduction	3
1	Historical perspective	4
2	Geography of the region	10
3	Vanished in the Vale of York	12
4	To the Holderness coast	15
5	Hull & Barnsley	20
6	A way over the Wolds	25
7	Losses in Leeds	29
8	Change at Bradford	35
9	North to Northallerton	40
10	Wensleydale	45
11	Return to Richmond	50
12	The prospect of Whitby	56
13	A trans-Pennine fatality	65
14	Darlington deadline	73
15	Branches from Bishop Auckland	79
16	Leamside and the lost main line	86
17	Closures to Consett	91
18	The twilight trains	97
19	Newcastle Quayside	101
20	South Tynedale	105
21	Alnwick and Alnmouth	112
22	The Border Counties Railway	118
23	A present of the past	125

First published 1997

ISBN 0 7110 2522 3

Code: 9706/B1

Published by Ian Allan Publishing, an imprint of Ian Allan Ltd, Terminal House, Station Approach, Shepperton, Surrey TW17 8AS; and printed by Ian Allan Printing Ltd at its works at Coombelands, Runnymede, England.

ACKNOWLEDGEMENTS
I would like to thank all those who helped me with this book.
In particular, I would like to thank my parents whose patience and understanding when I was younger allowed me to visit so many lines that are now closed. I would also like to thank all those courteous and helpful railwaymen and women who once worked on the lines mentioned in this book.

Cover photographs courtesy Colour-Rail

Introduction

This is the sixth book in the 'Lost Lines' series. As in the rest of the series, a cross-section of closed lines has been selected for this volume on the northeast, for their regional interest and for their wider historical and geographical associations.

In 1923, by amalgamation of smaller companies, the railways of Great Britain were divided into the 'Big Four': the London & North Eastern Railway (LNER), the London Midland & Scottish Railway (LMS), the Southern Railway (SR) and the Great Western Railway (GWR). When these private companies were nationalised on 1 January 1948, the new organisation called 'British Railways' was divided into six regions for management purposes. A separate North Eastern Region was established, the others being Scottish, Eastern, London Midland, Western and Southern.

Although there had already been some closures, at their formation the six regions covered one of the most comprehensive railway networks in the world. Yet it was clear, even then, that the changing trends in economic and travel patterns were no longer reflected in the distribution of lines. The problem was compounded in that, after heavy World War 2 use, the equipment on many lines was life-expired. Thus it was that the railways at nationalisation had extensive arrears of both maintenance and investment.

The ever increasing inroads of the car and the lorry meant that financially the railways were no longer in a particularly sound position and British Railways fell ever deeper into debt. As a consequence, in the 1960s notice was served that the complete railway network, which had survived relatively intact until that time, would be scrutinised as never before. The financial contribution of individual lines was to be examined and it was clear

from the then somewhat stringent methods of accountancy, that many would be unlikely to survive on a purely commercial basis. In a surprisingly short time the system was reduced in size. By the 1970s when the brake was eventually applied on closures, about 8,000 miles over the whole system had been lost, a length of closed line equal to the diameter of the world.

In the knowledge that change was inevitable, in the 1960s I started to record my travels by train and eventually covered, with a few short exceptions, every passenger railway line on each of the six regions. The railway network is now much smaller than when I first set out. There has also been much change both physically and administratively, and the North Eastern Region itself was the first to lose its identity. My subsequent visits to lines closed show that much still survives. Indeed, the earthworks and structures of abandoned lines have their own fascination, lost to the present, but certainly not forgotten

Abbreviations

ECML	East Coast main line
GNR	Great Northern Railway
GWR	Great Western Railway
H&B	Hull & Barnsley Railway
L&YR	Lancashire & Yorkshire Railway
LMS	London Midland & Scottish Railway
LNER	London & North Eastern Railway
LNWR	London & North Western Railway
MR	Midland Railway
N&DJR	Newcastle & Darlington Junction Railway
NCB	National Coal Board
NER	North Eastern Railway
NRM	National Railway Museum
RCTS	Railway Correspondence and Travel Society
S&DR	Stockton & Darlington Railway
SLS	Stephenson Locomotive Society
SR	Southern Railway
WCML	West Coast main line

Above: Map of the Regional Boundaries in 1958.
Ian Allan Library

1 Historical perspective

The North Eastern Region's origins are to be found in the very birth of railways. Wagonways were in use on Tyneside as far back as the early 1600s. In County Durham the Tanfield Wagonway was operating over the Causey Arch by 1726. Horse-drawn wagonways gradually gave way to steam railways and in 1758 the first railway to be built under an Act of Parliament, at Middleton near Leeds, received Royal Assent. The Stockton & Darlington Railway (S&DR) opened for passengers and goods in 1825 and was the first public steam-operated line. Traffic boomed as the need for coal to fuel the Industrial Revolution grew. A profusion of railways developed from the mines to navigable waterways and to the coast, transforming the region from an agricultural backwater to one of enormous industrialisation.

George Stephenson is acknowledged as the 'Father of Railways', but there were other pioneers from the northeast. These included his son Robert Stephenson, William Headley, Timothy Hackworth and George Hudson — the Lord Mayor of York and MP for Sunderland — who became known as the 'Railway King' because for a time he controlled almost half of all the railways in the country.

New routes and mergers were common, but almost all lines in the northeast were later to become part of one well-known railway company, the North Eastern Railway (NER). This was established in 1854 and the three main railways from which it was formed were incorporated into its crest: the York & North Midland, the Leeds Northern, and the York, Newcastle & Berwick. The historic S&DR was subsequently taken over by the NER, as was the first east-west line built across the country by the Newcastle & Carlisle Railway. At its formation the North Eastern Railway

Below: George Stephenson was born on 9 June 1781 in this stone-built cottage at North Wylam. A wall plaque erected by the Institution of Mechanical Engineers records that Stephenson became their first president. This view, looking east, was taken two centuries after his birth. It is perhaps ironic that the lost line of the Wylam Wagonway is located directly in front of the building. *Andrew Muckley*

was the largest railway company in the world. Although it was later overtaken by other companies, it grew and remained one of the most important companies in the country, maintaining a virtual monopoly in northeast England.

The NER's main wealth came from carrying freight, particularly coal. It opened Tyne Dock near Jarrow in 1859 for coal shipments to the south of England and for exports to Russia and the Baltic. It took over the docks at Hartlepool and Middlesbrough and purchased the Hull Dock Co in 1893. The NER eventually became the largest dock-owning company in the world. It also owned some magnificent stations, in particular York, with its great curving arched roofs, and Newcastle with its massive classical portico. Equally attractive smaller country stations were also to

Above: A 1920s photograph of a Bo-Bo electric locomotive hauling a freight train of up to 70 wagons, passing what is now Newton Aycliffe. The NER was a progressive railway that sanctioned a number of electric services, including this line from Shildon to Newport. It was the first line in the country to be electrified at 1,500V dc with overhead catenary. Ten electric locomotives were used on the route between 1915 and 1934, after which the line reverted to steam. The route finally closed in 1963. *Andrew Muckley*

Right: The coat of arms of the North Eastern Railway, looking rather like the figurehead of a sailing ship. This photograph was taken in 1996 at the former NER head office at York. The smaller crest at the top is that of the York & North Midland Railway, to the left the Leeds Northern Railway, and to the right the York, Newcastle & Berwick Railway. *Author*

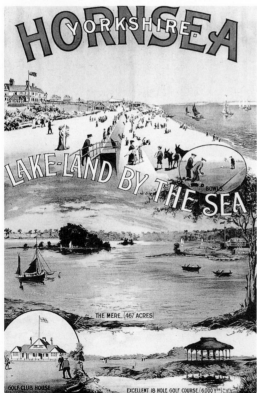

Above: The Zetland Hotel at Saltburn was designed by William Peachy. As this view shows, the hotel had its own private platform and rear entrance from the station. The Stockton & Darlington Railway created the resort and owned the hotel, which opened in 1863. The hotel has since been converted into flats, but Saltburn remains as a fine example of a Victorian seaside resort. *Ian Allan Library*

Left: A North Eastern Railway poster, aimed at stimulating travel to the delights of the Yorkshire coast at Hornsea. *Courtesy NRM*

Below: A NER 2-ton (2,032kg) chain-driven Commer lorry, No 67, used on Tyneside transhipment services and viewed here in 1906. The development of the lorry was later to have a devastating impact on rail freight. *Courtesy BR*

Above right: A view of Blyth staithes in August 1963. Such structures were the end of the line for coal trains from the numerous mines in the area and allowed the coal to be discharged directly into colliers. The substantial timber staithes have since been demolished. *V. Rayner*

be found throughout the area and the railway was unique in employing its own professional architects.

With running powers to Edinburgh, the NER operated over much of the East Coast main line (ECML) and in 1871 opened its own direct section of main line, south of York, to meet the Great Northern Railway at Shaftholme Junction. North of Darlington, ECML trains ran via Leamside until 1872 when they were routed over a new line via Durham. For many years, until World War 1, the railway provided the fastest scheduled passenger services in the country, on the line between Darlington and York.

Some secondary passenger services came in for criticism that they took second place to freight, although in 1903 the NER experimented with a petrol-driven railcar and in the same year became an early operator of road buses in Holderness. The NER also once had an extensive portfolio of hotels and refreshment rooms; today what used to be NER hotels at Hull, York, West Hartlepool and Newcastle remain open, but others at Withernsea, Scarborough, Saltburn, Tynemouth and Tweedmouth have all closed.

The NER was a progressive railway that was enthusiastic about electrification. The Newcastle suburban system was the first major electrified provincial system, opening in 1904. Later proposals to electrify the ECML between York and Newcastle were undermined by uncertainty brought about by the 1923 Grouping and many years were to elapse before this section was finally electrified.

The LNER came into existence on 1 January 1923 absorbing the NER. Notwithstanding that six main and

26 subsidiary companies constituted the new LNER, the NER was its most important, wealthy and influential constituent. Although the LNER extended from London in the south to Lossiemouth in the north, the northeast remained a distinct geographical sub-area of the new railway.

Of the smaller companies absorbed into the LNER, many were historical anomalies which had long since become part of larger railways. However, of particular interest was the Hull & Barnsley Railway. This company had tried to break the NER's monopoly to Hull, but was taken over by its rival in 1922, just prior to the Grouping.

After the LNER took over, freight remained buoyant, but the depression between the two world wars hit the northern industrial areas. This was followed by the ravages of World War 2, damaging railway property including the stations at York and Middlesbrough and leading to a general arrears of maintenance that was to compound the LNER's deteriorating financial position. The LNER was a proud company, but by the time it was nationalised on 1 January 1948 there was some relief as its ordinary preference shareholders had not seen any significant financial return since the 1930s.

Of all the regions established with the national-isation of the railways, the North Eastern was the smallest in terms of route mileage. The head-quarters were at York, where the NER had opened its head office in 1906, but the regional colour selected was unusual, tangerine, lacking any real link with the past. The regional boundaries chosen broadly embraced the area of the former NER; nevertheless, in West Yorkshire a number of ex-LMS lines were incorporated into the new region. (The historical background to these lines is contained in other volumes in the 'Lost Lines' series.)

The decline in the northeast's traditional heavy industry was reflected in the decline of the railways which saw continuous contraction after nationalisation. Much of the remaining infrastructure had also seen little in the way of investment and gave an air of neglect and dereliction. There was growing financial concern and after 1954 losses gradually mounted. In 1963 the 'Reshaping Report', which became better known as the Beeching Report, was produced. The remaining passenger lines in the North Eastern Region did not fare well in this report and one of the shocks was the proposed closure of all the remaining routes to Whitby.

Finally, in 1967 the North Eastern Region lost its independence and was merged with the Eastern Region, which remained in operation until it disappeared in 1991 in favour of other forms of management.

Today the network of railways in the northeast is very much reduced from its heyday, but the oil crisis of 1973, changing attitudes towards public transport, and local campaigns saved some lines. It is to be hoped that the days of contraction are now gone. There remains a great sense of pride in the railway heritage of this region. The anniversaries of the Stockton & Darlington Railway were first celebrated by the NER with historic locomotives that remain preserved today. Many museums have also been created in the area, including the National Railway Museum (NRM) at York, fittingly located in the region which saw the birth of the railway.

Left: A Thornycroft 32-seat bus of 1928, No 130, complete with its teak strip and acetylene lamps. It was operated by the LNER on services in County Durham. Bus services were to spell the end of a number of secondary passenger routes in the county. *Ian Allan Library*

Below: An official LNER photograph of the damage caused to York station by an air raid in April 1942. No 3 Platform was back in use the day after the raid, but the longer-term damage of World War 2 to the LNER's infrastructure was more serious. The repairs to the station are still apparent, particularly on the exterior wall. *Ian Allan Library*

Above: Class G5 0-4-4T No 67270 heads the 2.8pm Sunderland-Durham train between Cox Green and Penshaw on 19 August 1957, just prior to DMU working. The neatly planted bushes between the tracks, the heavily industrialised landscape and the branch line steam train were all to witness significant change. The Sunderland-Durham passenger service ended in May 1964. *I. S. Carr*

Right: The once attractive and substantial stone station house at Barton, seen here in May 1963 after closure of this freight branch which ran from the Darlington-Penrith line. The station buildings were demolished shortly after to make way for a road. *J. W. Armstrong*

Below: Bowes station, on the trans-Pennine Darlington-Penrith route. The station was shorn of all items of value and lingered on as a derelict shell, as viewed here in November 1971, almost a decade after closure. Following use as an agricultural store, the melancholy and dilapidated buildings were eventually demolished. *A. Muckley*

Below right: A number of lost lines have been reopened. The route from Whitby to Pickering is one such example. Here in LNER livery and numbered as 2005, a preserved 'K1' class 2-6-0 is seen at Goathland on 23 July 1983, passing an attractive array of ex-NER signals on the preserved North Yorkshire Moors Railway. The line runs for 18 miles (29km) between Pickering and Grosmont. *J. Titlow*

2 Geography of the region

For the purposes of this book, the boundaries selected are broadly those of the North Eastern Region at nationalisation. The region served an area that stretched from the coast to the eastern Pennines and Yorkshire Dales, with tentacles running over the Pennines themselves. It extended from the River Humber and near Doncaster in the south, to the River Tweed and the Scottish border near Berwick in the north.

The landscape was one of many contrasts. The bleak, exposed and remote areas of the Borders and upper reaches of the Yorkshire Dales; the Northumberland and Durham coalfield; the West Yorkshire industrial areas and parts of the South Yorkshire coalfield; the Vale of York and the scarps and vales of East Yorkshire. At Weatherhill, in County Durham, the highest point on the NER was reached at 1,378ft (420m), but from here a privately operated mineral branch continued to climb to 1,670ft (510m), near Rookhope and was the highest point reached by any standard gauge line in Britain.

The weather was on occasions bleak; anemometers were provided on exposed viaducts and the high Pennine lines could be closed by snowdrifts for days on end in winter. Heavy snow-clearing equipment was provided by the NER. Indeed, Wilson Worsdell, when Locomotive Superintendent of the railway, was almost killed in a snowplough accident, whilst a companion in the same derailed snowplough cabin was trapped under a cast iron stove and burned to death.

The area was rich in natural resources: not only good quality coal, but also iron ore and limestone. This in turn gave rise to considerable heavy industry, including the once extensive Tyne shipyards and Consett ironworks. The region served the Tyne ports, together with those at Blyth, Sunderland, Hartlepool, Middlesbrough, Goole, Hull and many other smaller installations. Parts of the Durham coast were stained black by almost a century of spoil tipping from the coal industry. Elsewhere the region served many coastal settlements. The larger holiday resorts of Scarborough, Bridlington and Whitley Bay still have railway services, but many of the more remote resorts such as Withernsea, Hornsea, Robin Hood's Bay, Staithes and Amble are no longer served by train.

The region contained a number of substantial engineering works. Some survive to this day, like the great bridges over the rivers Tyne and Tweed; some are part of Britain's lost engineering heritage, in particular the famous metal viaducts at Deepdale and Belah, which sadly were demolished after their closure. More tunnels of significant length were closed in this region than in any other, including two at Queensbury and Drewton that were both over one mile (1.6km) in length.

Below left: Belah Viaduct in 1955, with BR Standard Class 4 2-6-0 No 76048 and ex-LNER coaches crossing in the lonely Pennine landscape. This metal structure was one of the region's most impressive engineering works. Unfortunately, after closure of the line the viaduct was demolished in the 1960s, simply for its scrap value. Long-term plans for reconstruction and reopening of the line have been mooted. *J. W. Armstrong*

Below: Grinkle Tunnel on the line between Saltburn and Whitby, viewed here in the early 1960s after track removal in 1959. The North Eastern Region had more closed tunnels of significant length than any other BR region. As it turned out, this section of line reopened in 1974 and tracks once again pass through the tunnel and as far as Boulby. *D. Hardy*

Right: Map of the North Eastern Region. *Courtesy BR*

BRITISH RAILWAYS

NORTH EASTERN REGION

③ Vanished in the Vale of York

Immediately east of the Pennines is the low-lying plain known as the Vale of York, never exceeding 200ft (62m) above sea level. It is an important agricultural area and the city of York acts as a focus for natural transport routes. York is famous for its medieval completeness and its Minster. It is also a railway city whose Lord Mayor from 1837 was George Hudson, the 'Railway King'. He helped to develop York as a railway centre, and the first line to the city opened in May 1839 to a temporary station outside the city walls. Shortly after, a station was opened within the old city by cutting through the medieval walls. The terminus could not cope with the growth of traffic and by 1877 passengers were transferred to the present through station, once more outside the walls.

In 1906 the NER established its headquarters in the city. The attractive buildings remain in use for railway administration. It also established an important railway works there in 1884, replacing an earlier workshop dating from 1842. Unfortunately, despite a £50 million investment, at the end of 1995 the works officially closed, something which was blamed on a shortage of new orders created by the uncertainty of railway privatisation. However, the city's place in railway history continues today as York is the home of the National Railway Museum (NRM), which was opened in September 1975. It replaced the Clapham Museum and a smaller one in York established by the LNER in 1927.

To the south of York lies a lost stretch of the ECML across the Vale of York to Selby. This section of the line was opened by the NER in January 1871. It formed part of an improvement to the then existing circuitous route via Church Fenton. In common with many small stations on the ECML, the intermediate stops at Escrick and Naburn were closed in June 1953, whilst Riccall closed in September 1958, but closure of the main line itself was never anticipated.

As it turned out, this particular section of the line ran over the Selby coalfield and any subsidence caused by the subterranean workings could have been hazardous on such a high speed route. Consequently a new diversionary line was built and 11 miles (18km) of the former ECML, from the north of Selby to

Chaloners Whin Junction, south of York, closed in September 1983.

Today the closed section between Riccall and Chaloners Whin, which once saw north-south trains, has been turned into part of a long distance east-west footpath from Liverpool to Hull. The section south of Riccall to near Selby has been converted into a road. The station buildings at Naburn and at Escrick remain, as does Naburn swing bridge.

A second route that ran south from York to near Selby could hardly be more of a contrast to the main line. The Derwent Valley was the longest light railway built as a result of the act of 1896 which exempted light railways from certain obligations, such as providing road crossing gates. It opened in October 1912 from Cliff Common, northeast of Selby, to Wheldrake and the full 16 miles (25.75km)

to York Layerthorpe station the following year. Unlike the main line, the journey was slow and only during World War 1 did passenger trains run through from Cliff Common to Selby.

The railway achieved notoriety, firstly for remaining independent, both in 1923 and 1948, and by the fact that for many years it did not own locomotives, having to hire these locally. In 1923 a petrol shunter was purchased and in 1925 a Sentinel steam engine for freight. Two Ford railcars were acquired in 1924. These generally ran together, back to back, using one engine at a time. They were prone to vibration and were noisy, but in any event the line served a remote area and passenger services ceased in September 1926. The vehicles were sold to the County Donegal Railways in Ireland, where, suitably modified, they ran until 1934.

Left: Hole in the wall! Attractive pointed arches were constructed when the ancient city walls of York were cut to provide railway access. The terminal station within the walls was closed to passengers when the present through station, outside the walls, was completed in 1877. *Author*

Below left: York carriage works in LNER days. In this view staff are upholstering the seat backs for first class coaches. Workshops date back on the site to 1842, but a carriage works was established in 1884. The 45-acre (18.2ha) site closed at the end of 1995 and was sold in 1996. *Topical Press*

Below: An IC125 set with the 07.45 King's Cross-Edinburgh train passing Chaloners Whin Junction on 28 March 1978. The old ECML, to the left of this view, is no longer discernible at this location. *B. Watkins*

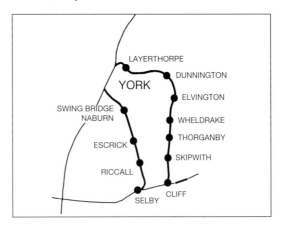

In 1977, over half a century after regular passenger services ended, a summer tourist train was introduced between York and Dunnington, in connection with the NRM. Yet the main revenue came from freight and as receipts fell the line was gradually cut back. The section from Cliff Common to Wheldrake closed in December 1964, Wheldrake to Elvington in May 1968 and Elvington to Dunnington in September 1972. The passenger experiment ended in 1979 and the remaining line to York Layerthorpe closed in October 1981. The former NER Foss Islands branch to Layerthorpe, which also contained Rowntree Halt and the link to Rowntree works, remained for freight until December 1988. Parts of the route have since been turned into the Derwent Valley Light Railway Path.

Above right: The former swing bridge at Naburn. Until 1983 it carried the ECML over the River Ouse and was in operational use until 1967. Today the control tower that was once located over the tracks has been removed, but the bridge remains and is utilised as a footpath and cycleway. *Author*

Right: Passenger services returned to the Derwent Valley Light Railway for the first time in 51 years in May 1977. 'J72' 0-6-0 No 69023 *Joem*, built in 1951, was used for a daily train of one coach and brake van and is seen here about to leave York Layerthorpe station. These summer tourist services ran until 1979. *R. Wildsmith*

Below: Dunnington station: the lightly-constructed buildings on the Derwent Valley Light Railway are seen here in April 1973. Freight services to Elvington had ceased in September of the previous year. *A. Muckley*

To the Holderness coast

The coastal plain from Bridlington to Spurn Head is known as Holderness. It is a remote and gentle agricultural peninsula of distant views and winding lanes. Parts of the coast here are the most rapidly eroding in Europe: the railways are also eroded from their heyday as two branches, with a number of similar characteristics, once ran to this coast.

The Withernsea Branch

The Hull & Holderness Railway was essentially a speculative venture promoted by a Hull merchant, Mr Bannister, as Withernsea was only a small village when the railway was originally proposed. The line from Hull to the coast at Withernsea opened in June 1854 and at first used the York & North Midland Railway's station at Victoria Docks in Hull.

In 1854 the railway also opened the Queens Hotel in Withernsea, next to the sandy beach and the station. The hotel and the railway were taken over by the NER in 1862, but the resort did not expand as anticipated and the hotel was sold in 1892. The expected substantial fish traffic also failed to develop, but from 1864, after the route from Victoria Docks to Hull Paragon station

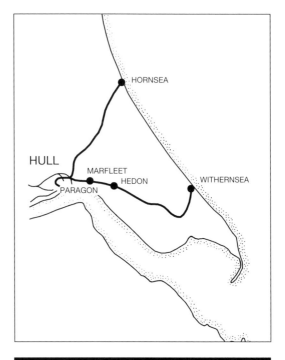

Below: Class V3 2-6-2T No 67686 pulls out of Hull Paragon station with a train to the Holderness coast in July 1959. Having once boasted 14 platforms, today this number has been cut by half, with an area once used by trains now used for car parking. The Royal Station Hotel, opened in 1851, remains and keeps its direct access to the station. *J. Haydon*

had been doubled, trains used Paragon station and a weekday service of about a dozen passenger trains in each direction developed over this 20.75-mile (33.4km) route.

In February 1927 a train using the branch was involved in a terrible accident. The Withernsea-Hull train was running late and the three signalmen in Park Street box, outside Hull Paragon station, were concerned that it should not be further delayed by the outgoing Scarborough train. In order to give the Withernsea service a clear run into Hull they set the road for this train, before the Scarborough train was quite clear. This resulted in the Scarborough train crossing through points on to the wrong line and running head on into the Withernsea train. Unfortunately, there was telescoping of coaches, 12 passengers died and many more were injured.

DMUs were introduced on the line in 1957 and patronage, which included commuters to Hull, was not insignificant, particularly in summer. Nevertheless, the end of the line was spelled out in the Beeching Report. The many level crossings added to the line's cost and closure came in October 1964, although freight remained until the following May. The station and hotel buildings remain at Withernsea, the hotel having become a hospital. Much of the line has since been converted into a footpath.

Left: By the time this photograph was taken in March 1966, the only double track left on the Withernsea branch was the Hull-Hedon section. Here 'B1' No 61002 *Impala* runs along this section, past Marfleet station, with the return early morning pick-up goods. A Hull Corporation bus crosses the bridge in the background.
Rev J. D. Benson

Below left: When this view was taken on 23 July 1961, a steam passenger train was an unusual sight on the Withernsea branch. Here 'Black 5' 4-6-0 No 45238 approaches Hedon station with a returning Chesterfield Midland-Withernsea excursion train.
D. P. Leckonby

Above right: Class L1 No 67754, based at Hull Botanic Gardens shed, shunts a train of empty coaches out of the main platform at Withernsea on 31 July 1955. Note the attractive ex-NER signals. Today the signals have long since gone, but the main station buildings, together with the former Queens Hotel buildings, remain.
J. F. Oxley

The Hornsea Branch

The Hull & Hornsea Railway opened its 13-mile
(21km) line from Wilmington, near Hull, to Hornsea
in March 1864. The main instigator of the line was a
Hull merchant, Mr Wade. He saw the potential of
Hornsea, with its sandy beach, as a seaside resort and
residential area. Construction of the line, which ran in
a generally northeasterly direction from Hull, was
more difficult than expected. Land in the Hornsea
Bridge area proved unstable and a viaduct, together
with some embankments, had to be reconstructed. The
cost of the line was therefore substantially more than
anticipated. Traffic also failed to meet expectations
and there was general relief when the railway was
absorbed by the NER in 1866.

Although Hornsea did not develop as one of the
more prominent resorts, passenger traffic grew and the
line was doubled by 1908 when about a dozen
weekday services in each direction were provided.
Services were also improved by the LNER and
although there was a summer peak, an effort was made
to increase regular commuting to Hull. No fewer than
12 intermediate stations were provided on the route
and there was a substantial terminus at Hornsea Town,
which included a five-arched portico that led towards
the sea. By the 1950s patronage on the line began to

Right: An LNER poster of 1931, by Friewirth, portraying
activity on the sandy beach at Hornsea. *Courtesy NRM*

HORNSEA EAST YORKS

LAKELAND BY THE SEA

ILLUSTRATED GUIDE FREE FROM COUNCIL OFFICE
OR ANY L·N·E·R AGENCY

decline and Wassand station, served by just one train in each direction on market days, closed in 1953, followed by Skirlaugh in 1957. As with the Withernsea line, economies were made: DMUs were introduced in 1957 and in 1960 most stations became unstaffed halts, but still the line was identified in the Beeching Report for closure.

It closed to passenger traffic on a wet day in October 1964, a far cry from the excitement of the opening day. Freight remained until the following May. A new government came to power after closure and in 1967 stopped the removal of the track pending a new plan for Humberside, but the prospect of reopening came to nothing. Much of the branch is now an official railway walk and a number of station buildings remain, including those at Hornsea Town.

Left: BR Standard Class 3 2-6-0 No 77010 leaves the swing bridge at Sculcoates and curves into Wilmington station with a nine-coach Sunday excursion train to Hornsea on 31 July 1955. *J. F. Oxley*

Centre left: The swing bridge at Sculcoates remains operational and in use as a footpath. This view was taken in July 1996. The design of the bridge is not dissimilar to other former NER swing bridges at Selby and Goole, with the distinctive control box located over the tracks. *Author*

Below left: A view from within the light and attractive overall roof at Hornsea Town station; note the hanging flower baskets and gas lamps. Standard BR signals in the far distance give some clue to the date of this photograph. *Ian Allan Library*

Above right: A view of the overall roof at Platform 3 of Hornsea Town station in BR days. The crossing gates once led to a turntable, but this was later replaced by one at the other end of the station. The roof has since been demolished and the area redeveloped, but the main station buildings have been retained. *Ian Allan Library*

Right: The station house at Hornsea Town was a graceful and imposing building set close to the sea. The building remains in good order today, as this photograph taken in June 1996 shows. *Author*

Below: The impressive five-arched entrance to Hornsea Town station still remains. Most of the former station buildings have been converted into residential accommodation. *Author*

5 Hull & Barnsley

Kingston upon Hull — better known simply as Hull — takes its name from the river on which a small and sheltered fishing port was founded; Barnsley was at the centre of the South Yorkshire iron and coal industries. The Hull & Barnsley Railway (H&B) (the shortened title came into existence in 1905) was an ambitious line that provided a link between the two. It was promoted by coal owners in Yorkshire and supported by Hull Corporation, unhappy with the monopoly of the NER.

The 53-mile (85.25km)-long main line opened in July 1885 and ran from a junction with the Midland Railway at Cudworth to a number of destinations in Hull, both in the docks and at Cannon Street, the central passenger station. The three crowns of Kingston upon Hull and the dolphins of Hull docks portrayed on the railway's crest revealed the fact that the line did not run into Barnsley itself.

To reach Hull the line had to climb and cut through a southern spur of the Yorkshire Wolds with deep chalk cuttings and three tunnels between Little Weighton and South Cave. At Sugar Loaf and Weedley the tunnels were relatively short, but at Drewton, the summit of the line, a tunnel 1 mile 354yd (1.9km) in length was required. In fact, the substantial engineering works required on the route made the railway one of the most expensive ever constructed, with capital of £4 million.

A number of branches were added: from Wrangbrook Junction to Denaby in 1894 and to Wath in 1902. Two joint lines were also operated, including one with the Great Central Railway that was constructed as late as 1916. However, the H&B was sometimes called the 'Hull and Nowhere' railway as its main line ended in a desolate mining area near Cudworth. It took time for traffic to grow; indeed, passenger services to Denaby never did, and ceased in 1903. A price war with the NER also had serious consequences on the finances of the railway, which for a time was in the hands of a receiver.

As might be expected, the main traffic was coal from South Yorkshire to Hull docks. At its peak, well over 100 freight trains a day used the route. Relations between the NER and H&B gradually improved — so much so that the great King George docks were opened jointly in 1914. Indeed, after years of rivalry the H&B was eventually amalgamated with the NER in 1922, just before the LNER came into existence.

The LNER thus inherited substantial docks at Hull with a total water area of about 220 acres (89ha) and 7 miles (11.25km) of quayside. Nevertheless, trade was declining; the LNER was

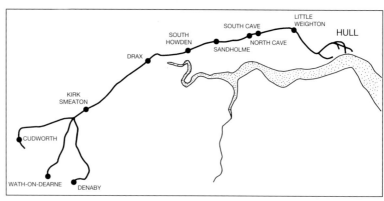

Left: To a background of the cranes of Alexandra Dock at Hull, WD 2-8-0 No 90482 climbs onto the ex-H&B line with a trip working to Outward Yard, on 9 July 1964. Alexandra Dock itself closed in the 1980s, but was reopened in the 1990s. *D. Hardy*

Below: One of the few surviving sections of the ex-H&B line serves Saltend, at the eastern end of the Hull docks complex. To reach this destination the remaining single high-level line crosses the River Hull on a swing bridge. This can be seen in the background of this view, taken in 1996. *Author*

Bottom: Timetable for Hull and South Howden services, July 1955.

forced to make economies and the H&B route became an early candidate for cuts. Passenger services to Cannon Street station at Hull were withdrawn in July 1924 and trains were diverted to Paragon station. The Wath-Kirk Smeaton passenger services ended in April 1929. Cudworth-South Howden services were run down and through passenger trains ended in January 1932, distinguishing the section of double track west of Howden as the first main line to lose its passenger traffic.

HULL and SOUTH HOWDEN

Miles		Week Days only						Miles		Week Days only					
		a.m	a.m.		p.m.	p.m	p.m				a.m	a.m	a.m	a.m	p.m	p.m	p.m	p.m	p.m	p.m
			S		E	S							S	E	S	S	S
—	Hull ....dep	6 20	11 45	..	12 20	1 15	4 30	..	5 18	5 55	8 30	—	South Howden ......dep	6 40	..	7 53	10 30	..	1 08	2 30	5 47	7 17	10 0
3½	Springhead Halt........	..	11 54	..	12 29	1 24	4 39	..	5 27	6 4	8 39	2	North Eastrington Halt	6 46	..	7 59	..	..	1 15	..	..	..	..
4½	Willerby and Kirk Ella	6 33	11 59	..	12 34	1 29	4 44	..	5 32	6 9	8 44	5	Sandholme	6 51	..	8 4	11 0	..	1 11	2 40	5 57	7 27	10 10
6	Little Weighton........	6 43	12 9	..	12 44	1 39	4 54	..	5 42	6 19	8 54	6½	Wallington	6 55	..	8 8	11 4	..	1 15	2 44	1 7	7 31	10 14
11½	South Cave	6 51	12 17	..	12 52	1 47	5 2	..	5 50	6 27	9 2	9½	North Cave	7 2	..	8 15	11 11	1 6	1 22	5 1	6 8	7 38	10 21
13½	North Cave	6 56	12 21	..	12 56	1 51	5 6	..	5 54	6 31	9 6	10½	South Cave	7 7	..	8 20	11 16	1 11	1 27	5 6	6 13	7 43	10 26
14½	Wallington	7 1	12 27	..	..	1 57	5 12	..	6 0	6 37	9 12	12	Little Weighton........	7 17	7 50	8 30	11 26	1 21	1 37	5 16	6 23	7 53	10 36
17½	Sandholme	7 5	12 31	..	..	2 1	5 16	..	6 4	6 41	9 16	13½	Willerby and Kirk Ella	7 25	7 59	8 38	11 34	1 29	1 45	5 14	6 31	8 1	10 44
20	North Eastrington Halt	..	..	..	..	6 21	..	4 6	4 69	9 21	19½	Springhead Halt........	..	8 2	8 42	11 38	1 33	1 49	..	6 26	8 5	..
23	South Howden ......arr	7 16	12 41	..	..	2 11	5 27	..	6 14	6 52	9 27	23	Hull ....arr	7 33	8 10	8 50	11 46	1 41	1 57	5 24	6 43	8 13	10 57

E Except Saturdays. S Saturdays only. For **OTHER TRAINS** between Hull, Eastrington, and Howden, see Table 23.

The line again came in for scrutiny after nationalisation. The last remaining local passenger services between Hull and South Howden ended in August 1955. The line closed to through freight in November 1958 and completely from Little Weighton to Wrangbrook Junction in April of the following year. The section eastward from Little Weighton to Springbank, at Hull, closed to freight in July 1964. On the remaining southern sections of line from Wrangbrook Junction, the freight link to Moorhouse closed in September 1963 and to both Monkton and Sprotbrough sidings in August 1967. The remaining line from Cudworth to Monkton sidings closed in September 1968.

Today short sections linger on, from Hensall Junction to the power station at Drax and the high-level line at Hull to Saltend. Many remains can be found on the closed routes, particularly where it was heavily engineered. Near Sandholme the track has been turned into a motorway and near Hemsworth and Willerby into a road. Parts are also used as footpaths and a number of the distinctive station buildings remain.

Left: This 1935 photograph shows the exceptionally deep Little Weighton cutting through the southern chalk tip of the Yorkshire Wolds and a 'C12' class locomotive hauling a passenger train towards Hull. *T. Rounthwaite*

Below left: Little Weighton station in the autumn of 1963, before the termination of freight services from Hull the following year. The earlier loss of the platform canopy is still apparent, but a number of platform lamps remain. *R. Pratley*

Top right: A view of Little Weighton station in June 1996. In private occupation there has been surprisingly little change over the years to the distinctive buildings. Although the track between the platforms has been filled, part of the line near the station is used as an unmade road. *Author*

Opposite centre left: With the NER already established close to the Humber estuary, the H&B line was forced to cut inland through the Yorkshire Wolds. This overgrown and disused section, viewed here in June 1996, lies to the east of South Cave as the line began its climb into the Wolds. *Author*

Above right: North Cave station in LNER days with a local stopping train from Hull hauled by 'A8' class 4-6-2T No 69869. The platforms were located at a high level as the line was on a steep embankment leading from the Wolds.
C. T. Goode

Right: The substantial North Cave station buildings still survive, including a clear notice indicating 'Down platform for Hull'. When this photograph was taken in 1996, the last passenger train had left for Hull over 40 years before.
Author's Collection

Left: The derelict Sandholme station in August 1975. After a number of years of neglect the buildings were returned to residential use. The M62 motorway uses this section of the ex-H&B line, running to the south of the station. *C. T. Goode*

Below left: South Howden in happier days, showing the well-maintained platforms and gas lamps. The platform canopies were later removed from stations on the line. This station, which acted as the terminus of passenger services from Hull for many years until 1955, has since been demolished.
C. T. Goode

Below: The swing bridge over the River Ouse at Long Drax was a costly engineering structure. It was being demolished when this photograph was taken on 13 December 1976. Note that a Bailey bridge has been constructed to carry cut sections of the open swing bridge to the river bank.
D. A. Watson

Bottom: Notice of closure, September 1955.

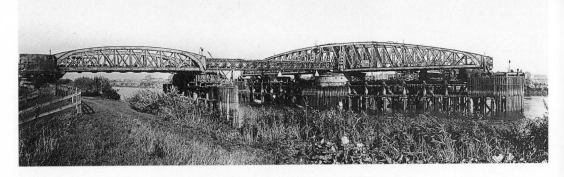

HULL and SOUTH HOWDEN

HULL ....
Springhead Halt .. ..
Willerby and Kirk Ella ....
Little Weighton ....
South Cave .. .. ..
North Cave ....
Wallingfen .. .. ..
Sandholme ....
North Eastrington Halt ..
SOUTH HOWDEN ..

The Passenger Train Service between Hull and South Howden has been withdrawn. An omnibus service operated by the East Yorkshire Motor Services, Ltd. is available.

6 A way over the Wolds

Market Weighton, in the Yorkshire Wolds, was once at a crossroads of four railway routes that ran to York, Beverley, Selby and Driffield. The first line from York, via Pocklington, to Market Weighton was opened in October 1847 by the York & North Midland Railway. The more difficult stretch through the Wolds to Beverley was opened by the NER considerably later, in May 1865. The two sections together formed part of an important 42-mile (67.6km) link between York and Hull and by 1889 the entire route had been doubled.

Services were gradually improved; the LNER even provided a connection at York with the northbound 'Flying Scotsman' and for a time a through service between Hull and Newcastle used the route. A refreshment room was operated at Market Weighton. The first level crossing in the country to be fitted with lifting barriers was installed on this line in 1953. DMUs were introduced in 1957 and in 1959 five of the least used stations were closed, but services to others were improved. There were plans to modernise the line in 1961. The stations at Market Weighton and at Pocklington were well located for the settlements they

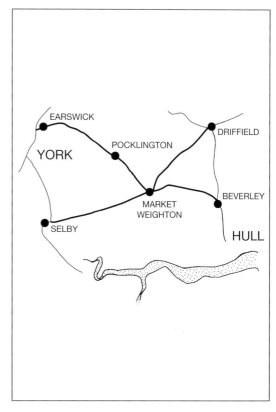

Below: A Bridlington-bound express near Market Weighton hauled by 'B16' 4-6-0 No 61428 in August 1957. This class of locomotive was commonly used on summer holiday trains to the coast. *C. Ord*

Above: The attractive and imposing restored colonnaded entrance to Pocklington station, viewed here in September 1995. Completed in 1847 and designed by George Andrews, it is considered one of the best of his smaller stations and is a listed building. When it was used as a station, two arches of the entrance porch were blocked off and converted to office space. *Author*

Above: The rear of Pocklington station is decidedly less elegant than the front entrance. The basic hipped-roof shed construction is apparent. The building is one of the few structures to survive on this line, having been taken over by a local school and turned into a sports facility. This new use safeguarded the station from the destructive fate of nearby Market Weighton. *Author*

served. New automatic barriers and signalling equipment was sent to Pocklington, the plan was to single the line and cut out most signalboxes.

Then the Beeching Report came on the scene. This selected the route for close examination. The report correctly indicated that the line served a rural area, with an element of commuting at each end to Hull and York. It reported that nine trains ran in each direction and on average there were 57 passengers on each train. The report went on to accept that the route's earnings of £90,000 more than covered its movement expenses of £84,000.

From these figures you might reasonably presume that the line was making a profit and would not be identified for closure. Not so. Add station costs for York and Hull, add the savings by not running trains at all and remember York and Hull could still be reached

by train. So now for the Beeching answer: by closing a line that ran at a profit, the financial improvement was expected to be £81,000. It is perhaps not too surprising that the Beeching Report did not achieve the financial results expected!

Local users were angry at the proposed closure, but despite opposition the line was closed on a snowy day in November 1965. The last six-coach train was packed with those who wished to say goodbye. Even then it was felt that the line might well reopen for freight and a single line was retained until 1969, when the track was finally removed.

My diary describes a trip on the line:

Monday, 26 April 1965; Took the train from York to Beverley, this is a nice branch and some of the stations retain their overall roofs. The

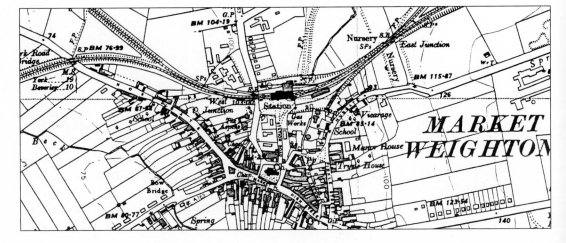

Above right: The attractive single-storey stone and brick exterior of Market Weighton station in April 1973. The stone pillars to the main portico were damaged by a lorry and part of the roof was displaced. In 1979 the buildings were demolished. *A. Muckley*

Below left: Map of Market Weighton station from 1908 with revisions in 1950. *Crown Copyright*

Below: Timetable for services between Hull, Beverley, Market Weighton and York, 1955.

lines at Market Weighton to Driffield are on ashes, as opposed to ballast, and were rusty because so few trains use them.

Today the once substantial station at Market Weighton has been demolished, but the impressive station at Pocklington, designed by George Andrews, remains and has been turned into a school sports hall. Considerable sections of the lost lines to Market Weighton have been turned into footpaths.

Table 18 — HULL, BEVERLEY, MARKET WEIGHTON and YORK

(Detailed 1955 railway timetable — columns of train times for Week Days and Sundays, with reference notes B, E, C, c, D, Dd, d, F, H, h, ia, J, J, K, k, S, L, N, P, R, T, V keyed to the services.)

Notes (right-hand column):

B Through Train between Bridlington and Wakefield (W.)
E Except Saturdays via Market Weighton. On Saturdays arr 7.32 pm
C Saturdays only. Runs 2nd July to 27th August
c Arr Darlington 10 15 and Newcastle 11 5 am on Mondays and Saturdays
D Saturdays only. Runs 2nd July to 10th Sept.
Dd Calls on Wednesdays and Saturdays
d Through Train Filey Holiday Camp dep 9 32 am to York (Table 25)
F Runs 27th June to 3rd September
H Through Carriage to Glasgow (Low Level) arr 5 9 pm (Table 2)
h Via Beverley. From 27th June to 3rd September passengers can dep 7 21 pm via Market Weighton
ia Through Scarborough (except Saturdays) Filey (Saturdays only), to York via Bridlington (Table 25)
J Through Train York to Scarborough arr 11 38 am via Bridlington (Table 25)
J On Mons. 13th, 20th June and 12th Sept.; and Fris. 24th June and 16th Sept. dep Newcastle 1 4 and Darlington 2 4 pm. On Sats. dep 1 4 and 2 0 pm respectively
K Arr Darlington 10 29 and Newcastle 11 23 pm on Fridays (11 7 pm on Saturdays)
k Through Train Filey dep 10 45 am to Leeds Table 25)
S On Saturday mornings 2nd July to 27th August dep Newcastle 2 48 and Darlington 3 44
L Except Sats. Runs 27th June to 2nd September Dep 8 12 am on Saturdays
N Arr Darlington 7 27 and Newcastle 8 18 pm on Friday until 9th Sept.; also on Sats.
P Via Beverley (Table 25). Dep 4 50 pm on Sats. 2nd July to 10th Sept. (3 31 p.m on other Sats.)
R Arr 46 am on Saturdays via Beverley
S or § Saturdays only
T Saturdays only. Not after 10th September
V Via Beverley (Table 25)

v Thro' Train York (Leeds dep 10 0 am on 18th, 25th June, and 10th Sept.) to Filey Holiday Camp Apr 12 29 pm (Table 25)
v Via Beverley. On Sats. arr 1 9 pm. On Sats. 2nd July to 27th August arr 12 17 pm
X Runs 10th July to 21st August
X Via Beverley (Table 25). Dep 1Y32 pm on Sats. July to 3rd September
x Dep Newcastle 1 25 and Darlington 2 12 pm 2nd July to 3rd September
Y Via Beverley (Table 25). Dep 11Y46 am on Sats.
Z Through Train York to Filey Holiday Camp arr 5 9 pm (Table 25)
Z Saturdays only. Runs 2nd July to 27th August Via Beverley
+ 4 minutes earlier on Saturdays
† Dep Newcastle 10 15 and Darlington 11 10 am on Saturdays

For OTHER TRAINS between Hull and York, via Selby, see Table 23
For LOCAL TRAINS between Hull and Beverley, see Table 17

Above: The melancholy and trackless platforms remained at Market Weighton in April 1973. The loss of the main train shed after World War 2 did nothing for the overall appearance of the adjoining buildings. The considerable scale of the former junction station is apparent, but it is a sorry contrast to the time when packed excursion trains passed through to the coast. *A. Muckley*

Left: Disused land on the approach to Market Weighton station, viewed here in September 1995. Today, with the exception of footpaths that use the lost lines and some former railway houses, there are surprisingly few remains at this once important railway junction. *Author*

7 Losses in Leeds

Above: A fine array of locomotives at Leeds Central station in BR days: from left to right, 'N1' 0-6-2T No 69483, 'J50' 0-6-0T No 68978 and 'A3' Pacific No 60055 *Woolwinder* on the up 'White Rose'. In 1958 the station handled 2.25 million passengers. *Eric Treacy*

Below left: A 1960s line-up of engines at Leeds Central Station with 'A1' Pacific No 60128 *Bongrace* and two 'Deltics' in their two-tone green livery on Saturday 18 April 1964. The last 'Deltic'-hauled main line passenger train ran in January 1982. *J. Whiteley*

Leeds grew with the woollen trade and heavy engineering, which included locomotive construction. The Middleton Railway put the area on the railway map very early indeed, with steam being successfully used as far back as 1812. The Middleton system lasted until 1958 when complete closure was threatened. In 1960 a section of the original route became the first standard gauge line to be preserved by volunteers.

The Middleton system was originally a mineral railway. The first passenger terminal at Leeds was provided at Marsh Lane. This station opened in September 1834 and was followed in July 1840 by one at Hunslet Lane; both were located on the edge of the city. Leeds was an important centre and by the 1850s was served directly by lines of the NER, Great

Northern (GNR), Midland (MR) and London & North Western (LNWR) railways. The railways fostered growth and the need for ever larger passenger facilities.

Leeds Wellington station, which the Leeds & Bradford Railway had opened in the centre of Leeds in July 1846, soon became part of the MR. The terminus was rebuilt by 1853 and the Queens Hotel, adjoining the station, was opened by the MR in January 1863 and extended in 1867 and 1898. The opening of the Carlisle and Settle line in 1876 made the Midland's London-Scotland route, via Leeds Wellington, a strong rival to the GNR.

Leeds Central station was used for a time by all but the MR. The station was built on an elevated level and some trains operated to the terminal by 1850, although building work was not completed until 1857. The Great Northern Hotel, designed by M. Hadfield, eventually adjoined the station, opening in July 1869. The hotel had a high-level covered approach to the station and boasted that its porters attended trains and the night mail. It suffered a serious fire in 1906, but the damaged upper floors and roof were rebuilt, the plain design contrasting with the original Gothic exterior.

Leeds New station was the result of continued passenger growth, and the NER and LNWR services were transferred there in April 1869. The through station was located on a site that adjoined the existing terminus at Wellington. Designed by Thomas Prosser,

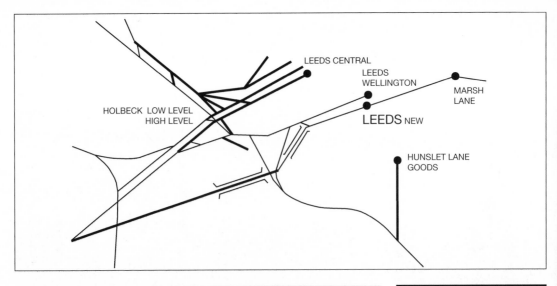

LEEDS CENTRAL

LEEDS WELLINGTON

MARSH LANE

HOLBECK LOW LEVEL HIGH LEVEL

LEEDS NEW

HUNSLET LANE GOODS

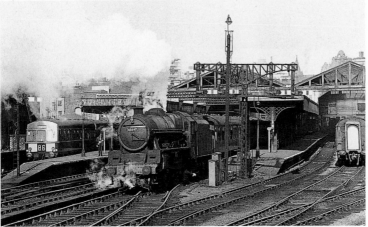

Left: Yet another change of scene at Leeds Central. 'Jubilee' class 4-6-0 No 45697 *Achilles* awaits the right away with a Doncaster local on 13 April 1966, before these services were transferred to Leeds City station. *L. A. Nixon*

Below left: On 4 January 1967 the 10.02 DMU to Harrogate stands at Leeds Central. The station would close on 29 April 1967, after the departure of the last DMU to Harrogate. *L. Dopson*

Above right: Fairburn 2-6-4T No 42145 approaches the remains of Holbeck High Level station with empty stock for the 6pm departure from Leeds Central on the last day of services. The Whitehall curve, built to let Bradford and Manchester trains use Leeds City station, is to the right of the train. The two Holbeck stations closed in 1958 and the lines through the High Level station have long since disappeared under a grassy mound. *A. Naylor*

Right: This attractive stone bridge over the River Aire once carried the line into Leeds Central station. The tranquil scene is viewed in April 1996. Although the river bridge remains, the elevated station area beyond has been flattened and turned to a number of new uses. *Author*

its most distinctive feature was the pair of mansard style roofs. New station also proved inadequate for the increase in traffic and an enlarged station was in use by 1879.

With the Grouping in 1923 the need for a single passenger station was contemplated by the LMS, who used Wellington, and the LNER, who used the adjoining New station. Financial stringency curtailed plans for a completely new station, but joint works were carried out. By 1938 Wellington and New stations were interconnected and the two stations soon both became known as Leeds City.

Most of the work was undertaken at Wellington

station and by 1937 the LMS had replaced the original Queens Hotel with the vast existing stone-clad building. The new hotel was designed by LMS architects in a mix of classical but mainly art deco styles. It was particularly advanced for its time and was the first in England to be air-conditioned.

On nationalisation, plans to concentrate all passenger services at a single rebuilt Leeds station were reassessed. Building commenced on the site of Leeds City in 1959, but cash ran out in 1961. After complaints, work was resumed on a reduced scale in 1963 and was completed in 1966, principally on the area of the former Leeds New station. The opening of the new station and track alterations allowed the remains of the former Leeds Wellington station to close in December 1966 and Leeds Central station to close the following April.

What remained of Wellington station became a car park and parcels depot, although there are plans for further redevelopment. Part of the elegant covered arcade area from the Queens Hotel was turned into a temporary car parking area. At Leeds Central station, apart from a wagon hoist from the adjoining freight yard, the entire area has been levelled and the site redeveloped. Yet much of railway interest remains in the city and both former railway hotels remain open.

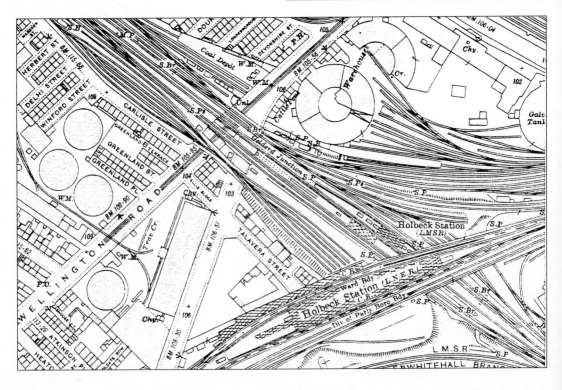

L. & N. E. R.

From_____

LEEDS
(NEW STATION)

NORTH EASTERN RAILWAY.

From_____

LEEDS
(New Station).

Above: Looking like some form of early defensive building, this railway feature remains near the site of Leeds Central station. The former hoist once transported freight wagons in the adjoining freight yard. When this view was taken in April 1996 a suitable new use for the old structure was being sought. *Author*

Right: A side elevation of the former Great Northern Hotel at Leeds, taken in April 1996. The 'hotel' sign is located on the truncated end of a passageway that once ran at a high level from the hotel directly to Central station. The top floors of the hotel, with their fine Gothic dormer windows and slate-ridged roof, were never fully replaced after a fire in 1906. *Author*

Centre right: In the late 1950s a Carlisle semi-fast passes the former Leeds City Wellington signalbox behind 'Jubilee' 4-6-0 No 45657 *Tyrwhitt,* with a train for the Carlisle and Settle line. *L. Metcalfe*

Below right: The spacious concourse that once provided a pedestrian route from the Queens Hotel to Wellington station and access towards Wellington Street. When this photograph was taken in April 1996, the magnificent and lofty hallway was used for car parking. *Author*

Left: Map of Holbeck High and Low Level stations in 1932. *Crown Copyright*

Above: 'Jubilee' No 45604 *Ceylon* at Leeds City with the 12.35pm to Manchester Exchange on 31 July 1962. Some demolition had already taken place, but the original mansard roofs had yet to be destroyed; the rebuilt station was not completed until 1966. *C. P. Walker*

Below: Map of Leeds Central station in 1932. *Crown Copyright*

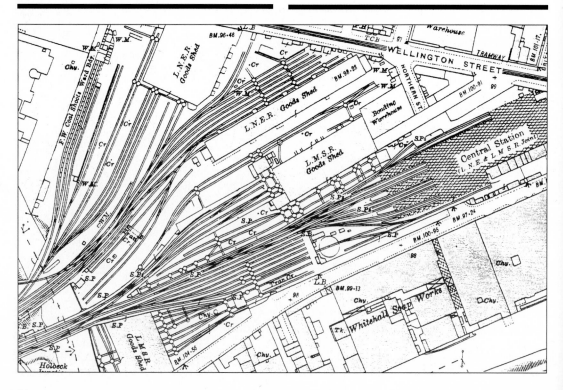

⑧ Change at Bradford

Located between the Aire and Calder valleys, Bradford was a major centre of the textile trade, and worsted wool and dyeing led to the city's rapid growth. Like Rome, Bradford is said to have been built on seven hills; one of the consequences of this difficult topography was that some lines in the area involved extensive earthworks. But topography could not be blamed for the need to change trains between the two main railway stations, Exchange and Forster Square. This was due primarily to a dispute between the two rival railway companies concerned — the Midland and the Lancashire & Yorkshire (L&YR).

The Midland Railway

The Leeds & Bradford Railway, later to become part of the Midland Railway, built a line to Market Street station, the first terminus to open in Bradford in July 1846. The station was extended and remodelled by 1890 when the Midland Hotel was opened on the site. One of the hotel's claims to fame was that the actor Sir Henry Irving died there in 1905. From 1924 the station was known as Forster Square and it survived — except for the demolition of the overall roof in 1953 — until 1990 when the original terminal facilities closed and a new station of just three platforms opened on a small part of the original site. In 1996 redevelopment of the remaining station area commenced, but the hotel — with the Midland's emblem of a mythical winged wyvern in the plasterwork — and the tiled walkway to the old station remain.

Below: Bradford Forster Square on 19 June 1990. The new station on the right opened in June 1990. At this time access was still via the old station seen on the left; a temporary causeway linking the two can be seen behind the train. Apart from some sections of wall, the remaining station was demolished in 1992, although the site was not redeveloped until 1996. The Midland Hotel still remains behind the new station. *R. Smith*

Above left: Map of central Bradford 1932. *Crown Copyright*

Above: An interesting wooden floor and tiled passageway was designed to allow platform trolleys to run directly from Forster Square station to the Midland Hotel reception area. The passageway remained, almost as originally built, when this view was taken in April 1996. *Author*

Left: An elegant stone screen wall graced the front entrance to Forster Square station. The wall remains but the illuminated station clock, which once formed a centrepiece on top of the wall, had disappeared when this photograph was taken in April 1996. *Author*

The Lancashire & Yorkshire Railway

The West Riding Union Railway, later to become part of the L&YR, had its own station at Bradford. This was the second station in the city, opening in May 1850. In 1867 the GNR also started to use the terminus and it became known as Exchange station. It soon proved inadequate and was remodelled and enlarged by 1888. Squabbles between the MR and L&YR prevented the construction of a through line to Market Street station and, although less than a quarter of a mile (0.4km) away, schemes for a link were never achieved.

With nationalisation both stations were eventually united in the North Eastern Region and the flexibility of DMUs to reverse in and out of Exchange station resulted in the concentration of services at this terminus. However, the structure had been neglected and in January 1973 the old Exchange station was demolished and was replaced by a new one 600ft (183m) to the south. In 1983 the new station was renamed Bradford Interchange.

The Great Northern Railway

The GNR provided a Bradford branch to a terminus called Adolphus Street in November 1854. At first temporary facilities had to be provided on the site as the construction of the main station roof, which was

Right: King's Cross trains await departure from Bradford Exchange station on 29 April 1967: Fairburn 2-6-4T No 42073 with the 07.15 and 'Black 5' 4-6-0 No 44990 with the 08.00. All steam working in the Bradford area came to an end in the autumn of 1967. *M. Dunnett*

Below: Bradford Exchange with one of its dilapidated, yet highly distinctive, fan-ended light iron train sheds, viewed here in July 1970. The two 100ft (30.5m)-span train sheds covered 10 platforms. In 1972 all services were concentrated on the former GNR side of the station to facilitate rebuilding. Closure of the original station site came in January 1973. *M. Dunnett*

originally intended to be of mansard design, proved problematic and the station was not completed until June of the following year. The final structure provided an attractive elliptical roof and the terminus was sometimes known as the King's Cross of the north.

Although Adolphus Street was an agreeable terminus, it was generally considered that its location, high above the city centre, was not very convenient. Consequently, when a heavily engineered loop line to an enlarged Exchange station was opened in 1867, the opportunity was taken to transfer all passenger

services to that station and use Adolphus Street for freight. Perhaps highlighting the poor location of Adolphus Street station, advertisements for the GNR's hotel in Bradford — the Victoria, bought by the GNR in 1892 — made it clear that the hotel was centrally located and linked to Exchange station.

Adolphus Street had a largely unexceptional existence until its closure in May 1972. However, in 1964 a 50mph (80kph) runaway freight train smashed through the freight yard retaining wall and landed in adjoining Dryden Street. Today, although some of the retaining walls remain, the station has been demolished and replaced by industrial units. So all three of Bradford's original passenger termini have undergone much change, but both the former GNR and MR hotels remain open in the city and retain many of their original features.

Left: Only very small parts of the former Exchange station exist today. This April 1996 view shows a section of the original retaining wall and facilities that were located at the south end of the station. *Author*

Below left: The interior of Bradford's Victoria Hotel contains some features that reflect the fan shapes of the former adjacent Exchange station. This view of the entrance to the hotel's dining room was taken in April 1996. *Author*

Below: Little remains of Adolphus Street today as the site has been given over to an industrial area and roads. This sealed-up side entrance in Dryden Street, recorded in April 1996, was a reminder of the scale of the former GNR station. *Author*

Above right: The exterior of Bradford Adolphus Street station, described in 1854 as being of 'modern Italian style'. Seen in September 1956, the legend across the pediment still indicates 'Great Northern Goods and Coal Warehouse'. The station and adjoining buildings were demolished after closure in 1972. *K. Field*

Below right: The gas-lit interior of Bradford Adolphus Street station in 1956, showing the striking barrel-vaulted roof. Note the continental wagons used on through services and the bales of wool. *K. Field*

The Leeds & Thirsk Railway opened a section of line from Ripon to Thirsk for freight in January 1848 and to passengers by the following May. Services ran south from Ripon to Harrogate by September of the same year. In 1851 the company changed its name to the Leeds Northern Railway and opened a line north from Melmerby to Northallerton in May 1852. The lines all became part of the NER in 1854.

The completed 25-mile (40.25km) Harrogate-Northallerton line ran in a generally northerly direction between Nidderdale and the Hambleton Hills. It crossed the River Nidd north of Harrogate and the River Ure at Ripon, where the line ran to the east of the city, including a section on a metal viaduct, finally crossing the River Swale to reach Northallerton. At first the main route to evolve was from Harrogate to Thirsk, with a connection having to be made at Melmerby, or Ripon, for Northallerton. By 1901 the line to Northallerton was doubled and this then began to emerge as the main line.

The LNER made good use of the Harrogate-Northallerton line as part of a loop, via Leeds, off the ECML. It was used by the 'Harrogate Pullman' and, when introduced in 1923, the London-Newcastle train included Ripon as one of its intermediate stops. By 1928 this service, which had already been extended to Scotland, was renamed the 'Queen of Scots'. Between 1928 and 1935 the 'West Riding Pullman' used the line, while in the years that followed other main line trains were to use the route.

Widening of the ECML in the 1930s led to a complicated series of junctions being provided at Northallerton, together with colour-light signalling. A new succession of spurs and underpasses allowed freight trains, from Teesside in particular, to reach the Harrogate line without having to cross the ECML on the level.

It was at this junction, on the spur that linked the Harrogate line to the ECML, in September 1935 that there was a spectacular near miss for two express trains running north together. Just as the train from Harrogate was running up the gradient to join the ECML, the driver saw an express on the main line also heading northwards at full speed. The train from Harrogate made an emergency stop — its Gresley Pacific being put into reverse and coming to a halt just short of the ECML. The other express raced past, having mistaken green signals at Northallerton station for its own right of way.

In 1955 the line north of Harrogate was still used by Pullman expresses and by through trains from the northwest to the northeast. The line was shown as a main route on BR maps and the historic city of Ripon still boasted refreshment rooms at its imposing station.

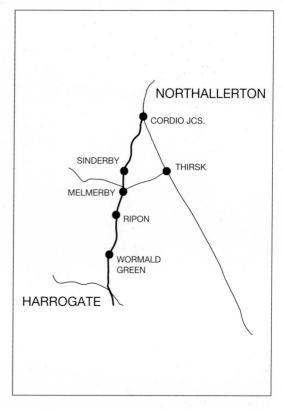

Although the line from Melmerby to Thirsk closed in September 1959, no one anticipated the closure of the main Harrogate-Northallerton route to the north. Unfortunately, all the lines north and east of Harrogate, to Northallerton, York and Wetherby were identified in the Beeching Report for closure. In 1964 Pullman trains ceased to use the line north of Harrogate and the run down to closure had begun.

The Harrogate-York line was reprieved, but the main line north to Northallerton, via the two surviving stations at Ripon and Melmerby, was closed in March 1967. Freight ran to Ripon until October 1969, after which the line was ripped up. Today a new road has cut the route at Ripon, but the Ripon Railway Reinstatement Association is active in enlisting support for reopening part of the closed routes in the area.

Right: 'Jubilee' 4-6-0 No 45562 *Alberta* with the Royal Train returning as empty stock from Ripon and crossing the River Nidd between Bilton Road signalbox and Nidd Bridge, north of Harrogate, early in 1967. The stripe on the cab denotes that the locomotive was not to run under electrified lines. *C. E. Weston*

Left: Ivatt Class 4 2-6-0 No 43057 near Ripon on 4 August 1952 working a down empty coach Starbeck-Ripon special, to form a return race special to the north from Ripon. This was probably the first occasion on which this class of engine worked a passenger train through Ripon.
J. W. Hague

Centre left: A brace of 'Hunts', Nos 62762 *The Fernie* and 62752 *The Atherstone,* double-head a return pigeon special from Ripon to the West Country on 26 May 1956. The heavy load of 20 vehicles is seen here on the 1 in 133 climb at Monkton Moor. All pigeon traffic ceased on BR after 1976.
J. W. Hague

Below left: A substantial and imposing stone and brick station was constructed for the city of Ripon and a refreshment room was provided. The station entrance provided three archways with the largest in the centre, a design that reflected the entrance to the cathedral at Ripon. At one time the NER provided a connecting bus service from the station to Ripon Market Place. The former passenger station buildings have been converted to residential use, as this view taken in June 1996 shows. *Author*

Right: Class A4 4-6-2 No 60009 *Union of South Africa* roars through Melmerby station with a northbound relief train on 15 August 1960. The crossing gates to the left of those in use are for the double-track Thirsk branch which closed the previous year. The points over which the locomotive is passing were for the freight-only Masham branch.
R. James-Robertson

RIPON

Above: The metal viaduct that once skirted the eastern side of Ripon has long since been demolished and a new road has cut the former line. Yet this stone abutment, just south of Ripon station, lingers on — a reminder that trains may one day return to Ripon. *Author*

Above right: An LNER poster promoting Ripon. The painting, by Fred Taylor, was based on an Aerofilms photograph. *Courtesy NRM*

12300

British Railways Board (N)
RIPON
PLATFORM TICKET 2d
Available one hour on day of issue only
Not valid in trains. Not transferable.
To be given up when leaving platform.
For conditions see over

Left: A DMU forms the 08.04am Northallerton-Leeds City train, seen here arriving at oil-lit Melmerby station on 4 March 1967. The service closed two days later. The former branch to Thirsk ran from the platform to the right of this view, services having ended in September 1959. *A. Brown*

Centre left: A three-car DMU passes the closed Sinderby station with a Harrogate-Northallerton local train on 19 September 1965. By the 1950s services to Sinderby were reduced to a single early morning train, and the station closed in January 1962. *L. A. Nixon*

Below: Class A3 4-6-2 No 60036 *Colombo* approaches Northallerton with the up 'Queen of Scots' express on 23 May 1961. Note the mix of old and new Pullman coaches. *R. Leslie*

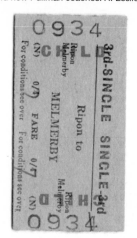

10 Wensleydale

The River Ure runs through Wensleydale, the largest of the Yorkshire Dales. This rural agricultural area is wooded in parts, but moorland gradually predominates west of Redmire. Before the railway, the Richmond-Lancaster turnpike road recognised the strategic east-west nature of the dale, as did George Hudson, who opened a branch from the York, Newcastle & Berwick Railway from Northallerton to Bedale in July 1848.

The route was extended westward when the Bedale & Leyburn Railway opened for passengers in May 1856. The extended line was taken over by the NER which planned a further westerly extension to Hawes. The Leyburn-Hawes section opened to passengers in October 1878, the line following the upper valley of the River Ure to reach Hawes, at the head of Wensleydale. The Midland Railway's line west from Hawes completed the 39.75-mile (64km) through route from Northallerton, on the ECML, to Hawes Junction, now renamed Garsdale, on the Settle and Carlisle line. With the exception of the Northallerton-Bedale section, the line was single throughout.

Although only a limited passenger service was operated, there was nevertheless some tourist use of the line to see the Dales landscape and attractions such as Aysgarth Falls, Bolton Castle and Jervaulx Abbey. The route also provided a useful trans-Pennine link and the NER had running powers over the Midland line from Hawes to Garsdale.

Rich valley pastures and the enclosure of hillside land provided agricultural traffic for the railway. The first commercial Wensleydale cheese creamery opened in Hawes in 1897 and milk traffic once operated over the line. Disused lead and coal mines still scar the area, but the stone quarry at Redmire was a lifeline to the branch that led to the retention of the route from Northallerton to Redmire long after other traffic had ceased.

The line closed to passengers between Northallerton and Hawes in April 1954. The section west of Hawes closed to all traffic in March 1959 and the Redmire-

Right: This view of Leeming Bar station, looking west, was taken in June 1996. Although the track looks overgrown, the section of line through this station, from Northallerton as far as Redmire, remains open for military freight traffic. *Author*

Below: Notice in 1955 after the withdrawal the previous year of passenger services between Northallerton and Hawes.

NORTHALLERTON and HAWES

NORTHALLERTON ......
Ainderby ..   ..
Scruton ....
Leeming Bar   ..   ..   ..
Bedale ....
Crakehall ..   ..
Jervaulx ....
Finghall Lane   ..   ..   ..
Constable Burton ....
Spennithorne   ..   ..   ..
Leyburn ....
Wensley ..   ..
Redmire ....
Aysgarth ..   ..
Askrigg ....
HAWES   ..   ..   ..

The Passenger Train Service between Northallerton and Hawes has been withdrawn. An omnibus service operated by the United Automobile Services, Ltd. is available.

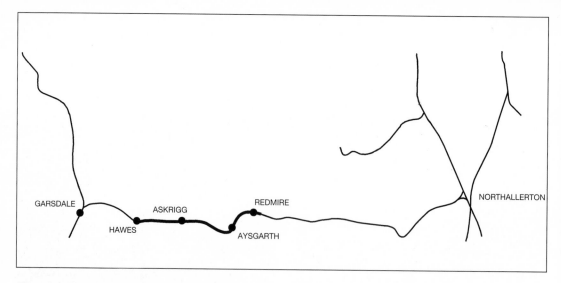

GARSDALE

HAWES

ASKRIGG

AYSGARTH

REDMIRE

NORTHALLERTON

Hawes section closed to the remaining freight traffic in April 1964. The line from Northallerton to Redmire closed to limestone freight in December 1992. However, trials for the conveyance of armoured vehicles on the remaining eastern section to Redmire, which is not too far from Catterick Camp, were conducted satisfactorily and the closure threat was removed. After track upgrading military trains began running again in 1996.

Stations still remain on the surviving 22-mile (35.4km) section, which operates as a very long siding, and some have been used for filming in James Herriot's *All Creatures Great and Small*, the TV series

about a Yorkshire vet. Much of the trackbed west of Redmire has been turned into a footpath, but stations remain. At Hawes the platforms and station buildings have been restored and are open to the public. In the longer term the Wensleydale Railway Association hopes to see passenger services restored over the entire line between Northallerton and Garsdale.

Below: In BR days a westbound freight train passes through Redmire station headed by 'K1' class 2-6-0 No 62044. *Ian Allan Library*

Above: On a rainy Friday 18 December 1992 Class 60 No 60086 *Schiehallion* poses for photographs in the quarry sidings at Redmire before leaving with the final train of limestone to the steel plant at Redcar. *I. S. Carr*

Below: The first station westward beyond Redmire, on the closed section of the line, was at Aysgarth. The bleak platforms are seen here, looking towards Hawes, on a misty day probably in the 1950s, although the photograph is undated. *J. W. Armstrong*

Left: Askrigg for Bainbridge station, looking west with 'G5' 0-4-4T No 67345 on a short Hawes-Northallerton train in BR days. *J. W. Armstrong*

Below left: Askrigg station, looking east in March 1973. Although clearly some change has taken place since closure, the main station house remains. *A. Muckley*

Right: No 61435, the last of the 'B16' class in service, running round its train at Hawes after an RCTS special over the Wensleydale line on 25 April 1964, just before closure. *N. Skinner*

Centre right: The iron bridge over the River Ure, to the east of Hawes station. The Ure, which runs through Wensleydale before joining the Swale, is famous for its cataracts that pour over limestone terraces at Aysgarth. *J. W. Armstrong*

Below: The station at Hawes was built for the Midland Railway. The stone buildings, after a period of dereliction, are now used as a visitor centre. This view shows the deserted platforms in September 1993. *Author*

11 Return to Richmond

The 9.5-mile (15.3km) branch line from Eryholme Junction on the ECML to Richmond was opened in September 1846 by the Great North of England Railway. From the main line, the branch ran generally southwestward to reach the River Swale and more precipitous landscape near Richmond. There were plans to extend the line further westward into Swaledale, but Richmond was to remain the terminus of the branch.

In 1910 there were six departures from Richmond on weekdays, with all trains running through to Darlington. The double-track line was used by the NER to experiment with fog signals, but the most notable feature of the branch was the growth in traffic associated with nearby army establishments. During World War 1 troop trains were frequently operated over the route, together with other military traffic. A 4.5-mile (7.25km) single-line freight spur was constructed from Catterick Bridge to link directly into Catterick Camp, serving what was to become the largest army encampment in Europe.

Richmond was recorded in the April edition of the 1956 *abc Railway Guide* as having a population of 6,165 and an early closing day on Wednesday. The guide also informed that the town was 247 miles (397km) from London, with the 3rd class single fare from King's Cross, via Darlington, being £1 18s 11d. By this time there were nine advertised weekday departures from Richmond. An additional through train from Richmond to Glasgow ran on Fridays, primarily for troops on weekend leave.

Moulton station became unstaffed in 1956, DMUs were introduced by 1958 and economies were made to the track and signalling, but as a classic branch line it was inevitably identified in the Beeching Report for closure. Despite opposition, the line closed to passengers in March 1969. Freight to Catterick Bridge, which was recorded as being of some consequence in my diary in 1967, continued to operate over the eastern part of the branch until March 1970. The vast army facilities at Catterick Camp remain and military freight may yet provide the opportunity for rails to return to the Richmond branch.

The station at Richmond was particularly attractive. It was designed by George Andrews and was a superb example of how stations were, on occasion, designed to blend in with their surroundings — in this case in clear deference to the nearby 11th-century Richmond Castle. Built in grey Yorkshire stone, the terminus provided a medieval cloistered entrance. A vast Gothic carved door led passengers to the single covered platform that utilised one of the two pointed-roofed train sheds. In later years the two storage sidings that were once provided within the covered part of the second train shed were removed. Almost all the other railway buildings on the site, including the connecting road bridge, were built in stone to attractive and distinctive designs.

Some time before the line's closure the local authority had informed British Railways of its interest

Right: An effort was made to promote the branch as this poster, in North Eastern Region days, shows. The text extols the virtues of the line's modern diesel trains. *Courtesy NRM*

		RICHMOND and DARLINGTON																						
		Week Days															**Sundays**							
Miles		a.m	a.m	a.m	a.m		p.m	p.m	p.m	p.m	p.m	p.m	p.m	p.m	p.m		a.m	a.m	p.m	p.m	p.m	p.m	p.m	p.m
					S			S		X	F	S Kk												
—	Richmond .... dep	7 38	8 42	9 50	1130	..	1225	1253	2 0	3 0	3 5	7 20	8 20	10 45	11 38	..	7 10	9 25	1240	2 14	5 56	6 27	8 20	10 0	1140
3½	Catterick Bridge	7 45	8 49	9 57	1137	..	1232	1 0	2 7½	7½	3 37	5 10	5 14	7 29	8 27	10 52	11 45	7 28	9 32	1247	2 18	5	2 6	3 48	8 27	10 7	1147
5½	Scorton	7 49	8 53	10 1	1141	..	1236	..	2 11½	11½	41	5 14	5 18	7 33	8 31	10 56	11 49	7 32	9 36	1251	..	5	6 6	3 58	8 31	..	1151
7½	Moulton	7 54	8 58	10 6	1146	..	1241	..	2 16½	16½	46	5 19	5 23	7 38	8 36	11 1	11 54	7 37	9 41	1256	..	5	5 11	6 43	8 36	..	—
12½	Croft Spa	8 3½	9 8	10 17	1155	..	1251	..	2 29½	29½	56	5 28	5 32	7 47	4 45	11 11	..	7 46	9 50	1 5	..	5 20	..	5 45	10 22	..
15	Darlington .... arr	8 10	9 15	10 22	12 2	..	12 5½	1 19	2 32½	32½	3 5	33	5 39	7 54	8 52	11 14½	2 7	7 51	9 55	1 10	2 35	5 25	6 54	8 52	10 27	12 9
247	2 London King's C'.) ... arr	1m3½	3½28	3½28	5 0	..	6 1.9½	3 18	7½48	9 46½	46	..	10 4	3 a 5	..	4 3½	5 53	..	5m40	4t30	7q30	7 55	2a10	3 a 3	..	4u35	5 53

a am	*m* Arr 1 13 pm on Saturdays
E or **E** Except Saturdays	*n* Arr 3 15 pm on 19th and 26th June
F Fridays only	*q* Commences 3rd July. Change at York
h Queen of Scots Pullman. Supplementary charges	*r* On Mondays and Fridays; also Wednesdays 22nd June to 7th September arr 3 2 pm (3 15 pm on Saturdays)
j On Saturdays; also on 13th, 20th, 24th June, 12th and 16th September arr 6 18 pm	*t* Arr 4 20 pm commencing 17th July
k Through Train to Glasgow arr 10 31 pm on Fridays	
u Arr 4 15 am 11th July to 5th September	
X Except Fridays	
X On Mondays and Fridays; also Wednesdays 22nd June to 7th September arr 2y10 pm. Except on Saturdays passengers can arr 1 57 pm by Pullman Car train. Supplementary charges	
y Change at York	

For **OTHER TRAINS** between Croft Spa and Darlington, see Table 2

in acquiring the station buildings at Richmond. However, despite every effort to conduct a speedy purchase after closure, negotiations were not completed by BR until 1972 and during the three years' delay there had been serious decay and vandalism to the buildings. Fortunately, after this period of dereliction the passenger station was turned by the local authority into an attractive garden centre, retaining many of the original features.

Above: Departures from Richmond, July 1955.

Below: Class K1 2-6-0 No 62005 climbs the Catterick military branch on 20 May 1967 with the SLS's 'Three Dales Railtour'. This 'K1' was subsequently preserved, but what a worthwhile line this could have been, had it also been saved. *M. Burns*

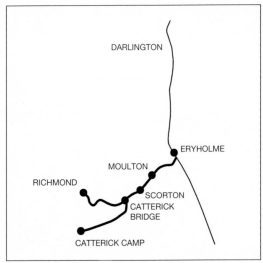

DARLINGTON

ERYHOLME

MOULTON

RICHMOND

SCORTON

CATTERICK
BRIDGE

CATTERICK CAMP

Below: An RCTS special at Catterick Bridge on 11 October 1952. 'A5' 4-6-2 No 69842 runs round the train. Considerable coal freight is apparent at the well-kept station. *J. W. Armstrong*

Bottom: Catterick Bridge on 15 September 1965, with a freight train hauled by 'K1' 2-6-0 No 62044, towards the end of the locomotive's life. A new waiting room has been provided. The station was severely damaged by an exploding munitions wagon during World War 2. Note that the station platforms were still oil-lit. *J. W. Armstrong*

Right: Returning with a freight from Richmond to Darlington during a wintry day in December 1965, 'K1' 2-6-0 No 62041 cuts through the snow as it passes Easby Abbey, located on the far bank of the River Swale. *M. Burns*

Right: The gas-lit interior of Richmond station in 1923. The station had its own gas-making plant. This period piece demonstrates the tranquillity that could descend on a country branch terminal in the periods between train departures. *J. W. Armstrong*

Below right: The attractive stone exterior of Richmond station in June 1968; designed by architect George Andrews, the building was completed in 1846. A notice informed that the goods station opened at 8am and closed at 5pm. Military personnel, who made considerable use of the line, are also to be seen. *J. Hoggarth*

Left: Class K1 2-6-0 No 62005 backs into the run round loop at Richmond with a railtour on 20 May 1967. There has been little real change at the station since the 1920s. The locomotive was subsequently preserved. *M. Dunnett*

Below left: Richmond station in June 1968 showing the pointed roof line. Electricity had at last replaced gas and DMUs steam. The considerable supply of luggage trolleys remained, but the sloping platform prevented them drifting on to the track. *J. Hoggarth*

Top right: Scorton station in April 1974, after closure of the line. The attractive stone building has undergone some alteration to provide for a garage. *A. Muckley*

Centre right: A number of railway buildings associated with the Richmond branch remain. At Richmond the terminus has been converted into a garden centre, seen here in July 1996. *Author*

Right: The road bridge over the River Swale linked Richmond station to the town and was also constructed by the railway. The design was again in an attractive, essentially medieval style and the bridge remains in use. A June 1996 view. *Author*

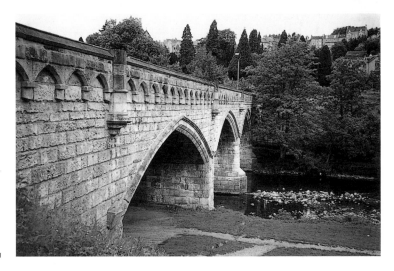

12 The prospect of Whitby

On the coast of North Yorkshire, Whitby lies surrounded by the adjoining dark heights of the North York Moors. Built in a ravine at the mouth of the River Esk, at one time Whitby was a whaling port and shipbuilding centre. Captain Cook's ship, the *Endeavour,* was built here in 1764 in a yard adjoining the site of the railway station.

The Whitby & Pickering Railway was the first line to serve the town, opening between Whitby and Grosmont in June 1835, and the full 24.25 miles (39km) to Pickering in May 1836. The original route was surveyed by none other than George Stephenson. For the first decade horses were used for traction; the line also entailed a rope-hauled incline at Beck Hole. In 1865 a 4.5-mile (7.25km) diversion, at 1 in 49 grade, replaced the incline.

The next line to reach the town was from the north: the Whitby, Redcar & Middlesbrough Union Railway which opened in December 1883. The 23.75-mile (38.25km) section from Saltburn to Whitby West Cliff ran close to the coast for much of its length and contained a number of metal viaducts, the 790ft (241m)-long and 152ft (47m)-high Staithes Viaduct, across the Dalehouse Valley, being the largest. Difficulties caused by landslides during the construction of this route resulted in the company

running into financial trouble and work ceased in 1874. The line was taken over by the NER which was obliged to rectify some inadequate construction before trains could operate over the line. After the eventual opening, George Hudson speculated in Whitby. He bought fields for new development on the West Cliff in 1884, near the new station. He successfully aimed to attract tourists from the northern cities, establishing Whitby with its holiday trade on which it still depends.

From the south, the Scarborough & Whitby Railway opened its 21.75-mile (35km) line along the scenic coast in July 1885. It was worked by the NER from the start and was absorbed into that railway in 1898. The line took four years to complete and included the brick-built 13-arch 915ft (279m)-long and up to 125ft (38m)-high Esk Valley Viaduct. The viaduct itself crosses over the Esk Valley line and a closed spur that once provided a link between

Below: A rather run-down Brotton station, looking south, on 24 February 1973. The station area is used for tyre repairs. Freight continues to use this part of the former northern coastal route to Whitby as far as Boulby. *A. Muckley*

Whitby's two stations. On the closure of the northern coastal route, the spur allowed trains to reverse into Whitby Town station from West Cliff station.

The link between Scarborough and Whitby was unprofitable from the start, in that the area it served was remote and the summer excursion traffic was short in duration. The single line was steeply graded, and sea-mists, resulting in damp rails, could lead to trains stalling on the gradients. Consequently, when the LNER took over, experiments with railcars were initiated on the coastal lines. In the 1930s, circular tours from York were introduced and this period was to prove the heyday of the routes, which could hardly cope with all the summer traffic. After World War 2 deficits again started as competition with the car and coach increased. Winter passenger traffic could be particularly meagre, and fish, timber and other freight from Whitby's port was also limited.

Economy measures were introduced in the 1950s. Scalby station closed to regular trains in 1953; Hayburn Wyke became unstaffed in 1955 and Fyling Hall followed in 1958. The section north of Whitby West Cliff to Loftus closed to all traffic in May 1958. DMUs were introduced on the remaining southern coastal route in 1958; they also found difficulty in handling the steep gradients. The short section between Prospect Hill and Whitby West Cliff station closed in June 1961. All remaining lines were identified in the Beeching Report for closure. The

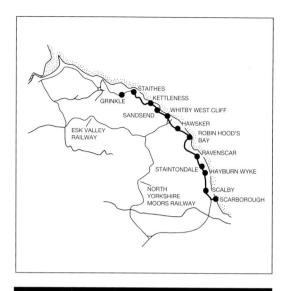

Below: From this angle the metal Staithes Viaduct looks decidedly delicate as a Whitby-bound train crosses with a Class A8 4-6-2T in charge. The 790ft (241m)-long and 152ft (46m)-high viaduct embraced an anemometer and wheel guides to safeguard trains using the structure in gales. There were originally concerns over the standard of construction of the metal viaducts on this route and after the Tay Bridge collapse in 1879 this structure was strengthened. *G. Oates*

Whitby-Scarborough line duly closed to freight in 1964 and to all traffic in March of the following year.

The line to Pickering also closed in March 1965, but in 1973 18 miles (29km) were reopened between Grosmont and Pickering by the North Yorkshire Moors Railway. The line between Scarborough and Whitby has been turned into a long-distance path, although there have been ideas for a narrow gauge line on part of the route. A section of the northern coastal line reopened for freight between Skinningrove and a potash mine at Boulby in 1974.

The remaining line via Grosmont to Middlesbrough had also been identified in the Beeching Report for closure, but enough was enough. The prospect of no trains to remote Whitby resulted in a fight and the scenic Esk Valley line remains open today. As for the future, albeit there are significant problems, a new link between Pickering and Rillington looks an enticing option as an extension to the North Yorkshire Moors Railway. A spur for Scarborough could perhaps be restored, offering once again the prospect of many scenic tours to Whitby.

Below: Whitby Town and Whitby West Cliff services, July 1955.

Bottom: The abandoned Kettleness station, viewed here after closure of the route in 1958. Note the substantial wall, shelter perhaps against chilly sea breezes. *D. Hardy*

Table 28 — WHITBY (Town) and WHITBY WEST CLIFF

			Week Days																					Sundays		
Miles		a.m	a.m		a.m	a.m CS		a.m S		p.m		p.m Y	p.m		p.m		p.m		p.m C		p.m Y		p.m		p.m	p.m
	Whitby (Town) ....dep	6 52	9 5	..	9 40	10 12	..	10 45	..	12 30	..	1 55	4 20	..	5 58	..	6 33	..	7 13	..	7 30	..	8 5	..	3 45	7 42
1½	Whitby West Cliff .arr	6 58	9 11	..	9 46	10 18	..	10 51	..	12 36	..	2 1	4 26	..	6 4	..	6 39	..	7 19	..	7 36	..	8 11	..	3 51	7 48

			Week Days																	Sundays	
Miles		a.m	a.m		a.m C	a.m		a.m S	Y	p.m		p.m Y	p.m		p.m C	p.m		p.m		p.m	p.m
	Whitby West Cliff .dep	9 29	9 58	..	10 30	10 54	..	11 25	11 57	..	1 1	..	3 23	3 35	..	6 28	..	7 45	8 22	..	9 26	12 13	3 27
1½	Whitby (Town) ....arr	9 35	10 4	..	10 36	11 0	..	11 31	12 3	..	1 7	..	3 33	3 41	..	6 34	..	7 51	8 28	..	9 32	12 19	3 33

C Runs 2nd July to 10th September   S Saturdays only   Y Not after 3rd September

Right: Ivatt Class 4 2-6-0 No 43071 on the 10.22am Middlesbrough-Scarborough train, between Sandsend and Whitby West Cliff, on 16 July 1957. *M. Mensing*

Centre right: Class A8 4-6-2T No 69886 arrives at Whitby West Cliff from Whitby Town with a local train on a wet August day in 1954. The journey between the two stations at Whitby involved a 1 in 54 grade and took 6min. The main passenger buildings still remain at both stations. *K. Field*

Right: BR Standard Class 4 2-6-4T No 80116 with the 8.57am Whitby Town-Scarborough train leaving Prospect Hill Junction after propelling its train up the spur from Whitby Town station on 3 May 1958. The northern line from Whitby West Cliff to Loftus closed two days later. The short section from Prospect Hill Junction to Whitby West Cliff station remained until June 1961. *S. C. Nash*

Above: In July 1957 BR Standard Class 4 2-6-4T No 80119 with the 10.44am Whitby Town-Whitby West Cliff train climbs the connecting spur to the Middlesbrough-Scarborough line, passing under the 13-arch, 915ft (279m)-long and up to 125ft (38m)-high Larpool Viaduct, which was also known as the Esk Valley Viaduct. *M. Mensing*

Left: The 12.30pm Stockton-Scarborough train, hauled by 'B1' 4-6-0 No 61030 *Nyala,* rolling along the short down gradient out of Whitby West Cliff with a five-coach train on 7 July 1957. *M. Mensing*

Above: Class A8 4-6-2T No 69867 with the 8.23am Stockton-Scarborough train making a laboured start with its five coaches on the 1 in 43 gradient from Larpool Viaduct towards Hawsker on 19 July 1957. *M. Mensing*

Right: In the mid-1950s, the single line token is about to be exchanged at the smartly kept Hawsker station with 'A8' 4-6-2T No 69879. *J. W. Armstrong*

Below right: Hawsker station viewed on 24 February 1973. The track from Whitby to Hawsker remained *in situ* because of the prospect of new potash workings in the area. As it turned out, the line was never used for this purpose and the track was eventually lifted. Hawsker station buildings still remain today. *A. Muckley*

Above left: The 12.50pm Middlesbrough-Scarborough train is seen on 6 March 1965, the last day of services over the route, at Robin Hood's Bay station with a lot of passengers on the platform. The signalbox at Robin Hood's Bay survived for three more decades and was the last to remain on the closed route. *M. Burns*

Left: The picturesque sweep of Robin Hood's Bay can be seen in the background as a DMU climbs the steep grade on its way to Scarborough in the early 1960s. *T. H. Mason*

Above right: The 4.02pm Scarborough-Middlesbrough train arrives at the oil-lamp lit wooden platform at Ravenscar, hauled by 'B1' class 4-6-0 No 61037 *Jairou* on 13 July 1957. On the left BR Standard Class 4 2-6-4T No 80120 is waiting to proceed along the single line with the 4.20pm Whitby Town-Scarborough train. *M. Mensing*

Centre right: On 9 August 1956 'B1' class 4-6-0 No 61353 emerges from under a road bridge on the single and remote coastal line near Ravenscar. *Ian Allan Library*

Right: Camping coaches were provided at many stations on the coastal routes and were well used until the closure of the lines. In LNER days accommodation for six cost £2 10s per week. Here at Scalby station the camping coaches remain in the siding prior to the closure of the line in 1965. *D. Hardy*

Left: The sad remains of Fyling Hall station after the track had been removed following the closure of the route in 1965. *D. Hardy*

Centre left: To the north of Scarborough station the old line to Whitby has been turned into a footpath, as this view taken in July 1996 shows. Although the route to Whitby was a single line, in the Scarborough area the width of the bridges indicates where a second single line once ran alongside the Whitby route to Northstead carriage sidings. *Author*

Above: At Scarborough the southern link from Whitby involved the single line 780ft (238m) Falsgrave Tunnel, which was situated next to the extensive Falsgrave signalbox. After closure to passengers in 1965 until closed in 1985, a track ran through the tunnel to the yard at Gallows Close just beyond. The former yard area is now occupied by a supermarket. This view was taken in July 1996, when Scarborough was one of the few large stations still to retain many of its semaphore signals. *Author*

Left: Trains still run to Whitby on the Esk Valley line and connection can be made at Grosmont for the North Yorkshire Moors Railway. This photograph is taken from a train to Whitby in 1967, running towards the vast disused Larpool Viaduct. It is estimated that the viaduct was constructed from five million bricks. *Author*

13 A trans-Pennine fatality

The Stainmore Gap between the upper Tees and the upper Eden valleys is the highest, bleakest and most difficult of Pennine gaps. Nevertheless, a trans-Pennine line from Darlington to Tebay and Penrith, with the intention of conveying iron ore from Lancashire to the iron industry on Teesside and coal and coke to Lancashire, was built in stages over the top of the Pennines at Stainmore.

The first stage was built by the Darlington & Barnard Castle Railway, which opened between the towns in its title in July 1856. The South Durham & Lancashire Union Railway then opened the section between Barnard Castle and Barras in March 1861 and the Barras-Tebay section in August of the same year. The Eden Valley Railway completed the link between Kirkby Stephen and Eden Valley Junction, south of Penrith on the WCML, in June 1862. All the companies were amalgamated, firstly into the Stockton & Darlington Railway and later with the NER, which was anxious to retain a monopoly in the area.

Thus was created a spectacular 64.75-mile (104km) trans-Pennine route from Darlington to Penrith. The line involved lengthy gradients and substantial engineering works, crossing the bleak Pennines and climbing to 1,370ft (418m) at Stainmore Summit. The high and exposed stretches of line were affected by adverse winter weather and some sections could be blocked by snow for days.

Originally it was a single line, but mineral traffic grew to such an extent that by 1874 much of the route had been doubled, which necessitated rebuilding many viaducts on the line. The viaducts were built to the designs of Thomas Bouch and concerns over their strength, after the Tay Bridge collapse, meant that weight restrictions were imposed. Although passenger services were sparse, the route from Darlington to Penrith was shown as one of the main lines on both LNER and early BR maps.

The inevitable decline set in: freight decreased and the area served was remote. The line closed in stages ending its trans-Pennine role. The Tebay-Kirkby Stephen East branch, which had become part of London Midland Region, was the first through section to close to passengers in December 1952, although occasional trains used this section until 1961. Closure between Barnard Castle and Penrith came in January 1962. The remaining service, which ran from Darlington to Middleton-in-Teesdale via Barnard Castle, closed to passenger traffic in November 1964 and to freight in April of the following year. A short western section between Appleby and Hartley, later cut back to Warcop, was retained until March 1989 for freight.

At Barnard Castle, where the eventual line ran to the north of the town, the substantial stone through station has been demolished, together with the nearby graceful viaduct which crossed over the River Tees at a height of 132ft (40m). The next iron viaduct over the gorge at Deepdale was 161ft (49m) high, but was also demolished. The greatest act of destruction was the

North Eastern Railway.

From YORK

PENRITH

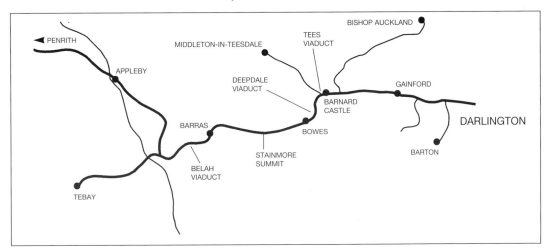

demolition in 1963, again simply for its scrap value, of the huge 1,040ft (317m)-long wrought-iron viaduct at Belah. This elegant structure had 16 delicate pylon-like supports of great beauty and reached a height of almost 200ft (61m) at its maximum, higher than any other in England.

At the summit at Stainmore part of the route has been turned into a road, while other sections are used as footpaths. The Eden Valley Railway Society aims to operate over a section of the line from Appleby East to Warcop and in the longer term back towards Belah.

Above: In this view of Barnard Castle station, looking west, Class V3 2-6-2T No 67652 attracts attention on a wet and clearly cold day in May 1952. The station boasted a well-protected platform and a refreshment room. *J. W. Armstrong*

Below: After closure, the handsome stone Barnard Castle station became a ruin. However, unlike the original terminus station in the town, part of which was saved and transferred to gardens at Saltburn, the later station was completely demolished. This view, looking east, was taken before that event, in November 1971. *A. Muckley*

Left: Having just left Barnard Castle, a DMU crosses the elegant viaduct over the River Tees on 14 November 1964. This viaduct, engineered by Thomas Bouch, was 732ft (223m) long and 132ft (40m) high. With the exception of the two riverbank stone abutments, the graceful structure was demolished after closure of the line. *M. Burns*

Below left: Ivatt Class 2 2-6-0 No 46481 on the 10.10am Darlington-Penrith train crossing Bouch's iron girder Deepdale Viaduct, near Barnard Castle. The viaduct was 740ft (226m) long, up to 161ft (49m) high and had 11 spans. The wooden decking necessitated fire precautions and buckets of water were kept at intervals along it. Two trains were not allowed to pass on the viaduct and speed and weight restrictions were enforced. The viaduct was demolished after closure of the line. *W. A. Camwell*

Top right: The derelict and haunting Bowes station, looking towards Barnard Castle in November 1971, before demolition of the crumbling remains took place. *A. Muckley*

Centre right: Stainmore Summit with Class J21 0-6-0 No 65033 at the head of an RCTS special train, westbound for Kirkby Stephen on 7 May 1960. This locomotive was the last of the class and was subsequently preserved. *Ian Allan Library*

Right: Ivatt Class 4 No 43018, with a banking engine at the rear, climbs towards the remote Stainmore Summit with a westbound coke train bound for Cumbria in BR days. *C. Ord*

Left: A view of Belah Viaduct with a freight train bound for West Auckland, hauled by Ivatt Class 2 No 46422 and assisted at the rear by Ivatt Class 4 No 43018, on 28 May 1960. Bouch's iron masterpiece — 1,040ft (317m) long and almost 200ft (61m) tall — was the highest such structure in England. It was demolished in 1963 after closure of the route.
J. Spencer Gilks

Centre left: The desolate Bleath Gill cutting, east of Barras, with a Penrith-Darlington train hauled by BR Class 3 No 77013 on 17 August 1954. The altitude of the line here and its exposed position could result in blockages by snow in winter. In 1955 the British Transport Film *Snowdrift at Bleath Gill* captured the bleak winter weather at this location. *J. W. Armstrong*

Below: Barras station, looking west, after heavy snow in 1947. Drifts during this winter reached the top of some signal posts in the northeast. *Courtesy BR*

Right: Timetable for Darlington, Kirkby Stephen and Penrith services, July 1955.

Below: Barras station with Ivatt Class 2 No 46477 and BR Standard Class 3 double-heading a Penrith-Darlington train in less adverse weather conditions in the mid-1950s.
J. W. Armstrong

Table 55   **DARLINGTON, KIRKBY STEPHEN and PENRITH**

Above: The closed Barras station, looking west, in January 1976. Note the recovery of sleepers. *A. Muckley*

Below: Class 25 No 7598, in two-tone green livery, with a freight train on the last remaining section of line from Appleby to Hartley on 15 September 1971. This section of the former NER line became part of the LMR and freight ran to Warcop until 1989. Kirkby Stephen East station is immediately beyond the overbridge in the background. *S. Creer*

14 Darlington deadline

The construction of the Stockton & Darlington Railway (S&DR), the first public line to employ steam power from its opening, was the dawn of a worldwide transport revolution. The closed sections of the original route are therefore of particular significance.

Coal was plentiful near Darlington, but the area was too undulating for easy canal construction. Consequently in 1821 George Stephenson was secured by Edward Pease, an influential Darlington merchant and Quaker, as engineer to the S&DR. In four years a 25-mile (40.25km) line was built from Witton Park, above Shildon, to Stockton Quay. The gauge selected was 4ft 8in (1.42m); an additional 0.5in (1.27cm) was added later to reduce friction. This choice of gauge was used on all the routes Stephenson surveyed and by exporting locomotives the British standard gauge was established throughout the world.

When Stephenson rode on the first train in September 1825 about 40,000 spectators saw the train pull in to Stockton Quay, to a 21-gun salute. However, not all were entirely friendly towards the new line with its noisy engines, and the first protest movement was established.

The railway provided the track on which private passenger operators were allowed to run. The single line was therefore shared by steam-hauled goods trains and independent horse-drawn coaches. The passenger franchises lasted eight years until 1833, when the railway took over the operation of all traffic and introduced regular steam-hauled passenger trains and fixed stations.

Above: The rather sombre-looking plaque affixed to the front of No 48 Bridge Road at Stockton-on-Tees, commemorating where the first passenger on the S&DR was booked. As with stage coach practice, the first passengers would have also been able to purchase their tickets at local inns. *Courtesy BR*

Below: St John's Crossing at Stockton-on-Tees in 1925, looking towards the riverside. The building to the right is No 48 Bridge Road. It was here at St John's Well that the first rail on the line was laid in May 1822. No 48 Bridge Road pre-dated this event and is the only structure remaining today. *Ken Hoole Collection (Darlington Railway Museum)*

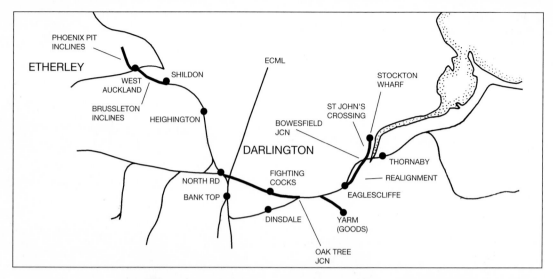

Left: No 48 Bridge Road in November 1996. The commemorative plaque was much weathered, but the building had been recently restored. The figure with crutches is the author, who had broken his foot running to catch a train! *B. Watson*

Below: Part of the Stockton Railway Heritage Trail, looking towards Bowesfield Junction to the south of Stockton. The quiet and tranquil rural scene, viewed here in October 1996, belies the past industrialisation of this area. *Author*

In the case of the original 1825 S&DR route, lost sections and stations occurred early on in its history. The first station at Bridge Road, Stockton, fell into disuse when South Stockton opened in 1836, although freight to the staithes survived until the 1960s. Much of the Eaglescliffe-Stockton section was realigned in 1852-3. Above Shildon, although short freight spurs remained for many years at Shildon and West Auckland, services on the Etherley incline ended in the 1840s. By October 1858 both passenger and freight services had been diverted off the rope-operated Brusselton incline.

The junction station for the Yarm spur was closed in June 1862. Fighting Cocks station closed to passengers in July 1887 when a new line, allowing direct access to Darlington Bank Top station from Oak Tree Junction via Dinsdale, came into use. The original section of line, which from 1844 involved a flat crossing of the ECML to reach Darlington North Road station, remained for freight traffic until May 1967. Fighting Cocks station closed to freight in March 1964, although a depot and sidings at Darlington continued to make use of part of an eastern section of the old line from Oak Tree Junction until 1988.

Every 50 years the opening of the S&DR is celebrated. In 1975 the 150th anniversary event was centred on the works at Shildon, which had been established by the S&DR in 1831. By 1975 the works was concentrating on wagon construction, but in 1983 closure was announced and despite protests, the works ceased all operations the following year.

Change continues, but the historic significance of the S&DR is increasingly recognised. Today it is possible to walk along parts of the original closed route, for instance at Etherley, Brusselton, Preston Park and Stockton. There are also many remains from the closed sections; examples include No 48 Bridge Road at Stockton-on-Tees, reputed to be the first real ticket office, and the first iron bridge on the line is preserved at the NRM. There are also railway museums at Shildon, Darlington and at Stockton-on-Tees. The aptly named Heritage line runs passenger services over the remaining original route.

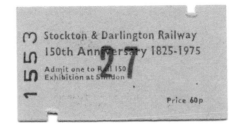

Right: Source of the S&DR. Witton Park, 1923.
Crown Copyright

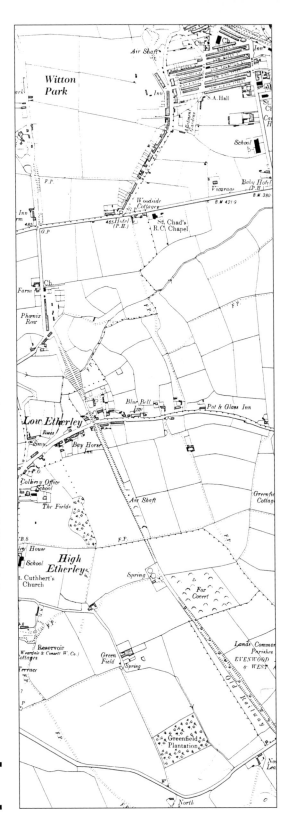

Left: The River Tees at Stockton where the S&DR once reached the bank. The old riverside wharves, staithes, shipyards and warehouses that at one time made up the port of Stockton have disappeared along this stretch of river. This view, looking north, was taken from the Victoria Bridge in October 1996. *Author*

Below: Fighting Cocks station on 31 July 1963. The track, signalbox and gates have gone, but the main station buildings remain. *Ken Hoole Collection (Darlington Railway Museum)*

Left: Fighting Cocks station, on a disused section of the original S&DR route, seen here on a dull July day in 1996. The station closed to passengers as far back as 1887. *Author*

Right: Class J25 0-6-0 No 1979 at the S&DR crossing north of Darlington Bank Top station in July 1939. The closure of the route via Fighting Cocks obviated the need for regular passenger trains to use this flat crossing with the ECML. Nevertheless, a single line flat crossing existed here until May 1967. *J. W. Armstrong*

Below right: Darlington North Road station looking towards Bishop Auckland on a murky December day in 1972. The original station near this site was replaced by these buildings in 1842. At one time the future of this station also looked bleak, as it was identified in the Beeching Report for closure. Fortunately, common sense prevailed and the line and station were reprieved. The station was restored by 1975 for the 150th anniversary of the S&DR. Today it houses a fine collection of engines and other items associated with the area. *A. Muckley*

Below: Extensive sidings full of wagons and brake vans awaiting repair at Shildon, looking west, in February 1984. Today most of the activity at this location has gone. With the closure of Shildon Works, only a single siding now branches off to the left of Shildon station. The siding is used in association with the Timothy Hackworth Museum, which is based around the old Soho Engine Works. *A. Muckley*

Above: Where the grade became too steep for early locomotives, rope-hauled inclines were required. This view shows the former S&DR houses at the Brusselton incline, above Shildon, which was worked from 1825 to 1858. The building nearest is the former winding house, then the engineman's house. The adjoining cottages are of a later date and were sold by auction in 1983. The area is viewed here in October 1983. *A. Muckley*

Left: A considerable length of the original track was still visible in the grass when this view was taken on a closed section to the west of Brusselton incline prior to 1925. *Ken Hoole Collection (Darlington Railway Museum)*

Below left: Original S&DR track on stone blocks, looking west over two bridges on a closed section of original line near Brusselton prior to 1925. *Ken Hoole Collection (Darlington Railway Museum)*

15 Branches from Bishop Auckland

The Bishops of Durham traditionally reside at Auckland Palace. The rural area was transformed by the development of the coalfield in south Durham, and Bishop Auckland became a focus for railways. A northwesterly extension of the S&DR, opening through Shildon Tunnel in April 1842, ran to within a mile of Bishop Auckland, but the first passenger line into the town itself resulted from a continuation of this route northward to Crook in November 1843. The Bishop Auckland-Leamside line opened, via Durham, in April 1857 and included three significant stone viaducts, including the Newton Cap Viaduct on the northern outskirts of Bishop Auckland. The route between Bishop Auckland and Barnard Castle opened in August 1863. By December 1885 the passenger link to Spennymoor was in operation.

As a consequence Bishop Auckland became the hub of a network of lines and a substantial station, designed by Thomas Prosser, was eventually provided. Passenger services ran eastward some 9.5 miles (15.3km) via Spennymoor to Ferryhill. Freight could also travel to Stockton via Shildon on a mineral line that between 1915 and 1934 was operated by electric traction. Services ran 21.5 miles (34.6km) northwards to Blackhill and some 25.25 miles (40.6km) northwestward via Stanhope to Wearhead on the

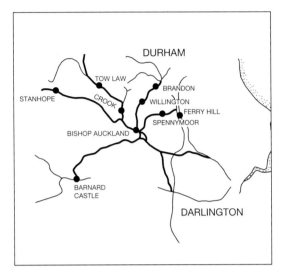

Below: This view of the signal gantry at the north end of Bishop Auckland station was taken on 4 May 1962, from near the North signalbox. In the foreground the Durham line is to be seen on the right and goods yard tracks on the left. *I. S. Carr*

Weardale line. A line ran 11 miles (17.7km) to Durham and on to Sunderland, via Leamside. The line to Durham, together with the 12.5-mile (20.1km) line to Darlington, provided a diversionary route for the ECML. The 15-mile (24.1km) branch to Barnard Castle allowed connections to be made westward over the Pennines.

The fortunes of the town were closely linked to the prosperity of the south Durham coalfield and the railway. As both declined, the list of lost lines grew. The passenger service from Bishop Auckland to Blackhill was cut back to Tow Law in May 1939 and that to Spennymoor closed to all but excursion trains in December of the same year. A number of other closures came prior to the Beeching era, with the accelerating decline of the traditional industries in the area. The Bishop Auckland-Wearhead passenger service ended in June 1953, although the last freight train to the Eastgate Cement Works on this line ran in March 1993. In June 1956 the passenger service to Tow Law was cut back to Crook.

The remaining services were identified in the Beeching Report for closure. All services to Barnard Castle ended in June 1962. Passenger services to Durham ended in May 1964 and freight four years later. All services to Crook ended in June 1965, together with remaining freight to Tow Law. Freight via Spennymoor to Ferryhill ended the following year. After a fight the line to Darlington was retained, although the substantial Bishop Auckland station was demolished.

Much remains on the closed routes. At Newton Cap the viaduct on the line to Durham has been converted to road traffic. The Spennymoor-Bishop Auckland route is now a footpath, together with much of the line to Durham. The Weardale Railway has purchased the 19-mile (30.6km) route between Bishop Auckland and Eastgate. Passenger trains still run to Bishop Auckland from Darlington on part of the Heritage line.

Left: An April 1973 view of the old tiled passageway at Bishop Auckland station, unchanged since the 1930s if the LNER initials at the top of the poster board are anything to go by. *A. Muckley*

Below left: Bishop Auckland station showing the gas-lit passageway in March 1976, before the station was demolished. *A. Muckley*

Above right: The 4.15pm on 16 June 1962 was the last train to Barnard Castle from Bishop Auckland. The train — seen here rounding the sharp curve to West Auckland — was made up of no less than seven coaches, but there were only a small number of passengers. *M. Dunnett*

Right: Bishop Auckland was a junction for many lines and had a triangular arrangement of platforms. This view, looking towards Crook, shows one of the disused platforms in September 1972. *A. Muckley*

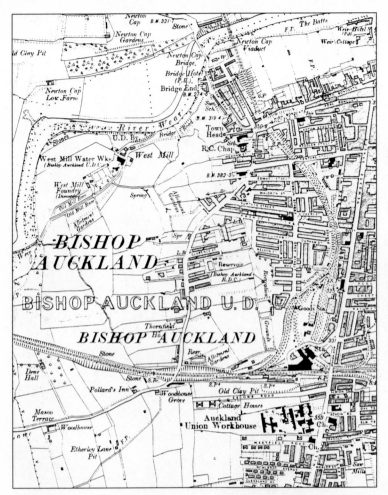

Left: Bishop Auckland station area in 1923. *Crown Copyright*

Below: A disused part of the station at Bishop Auckland was being demolished on 20 July 1981 when this photograph was taken of a Class 37 passing on the Weardale line to Eastgate. *R. King*

Right: 'Pacer' units on the 08.10 train from Saltburn arrive at Bishop Auckland on Sunday 15 June 1986. At this time a new station was being built adjacent to the Weardale line at Bishop Auckland. Much of the former station area has now been given over to other uses. *I. S. Carr*

Below right: Newton Cap Viaduct over the River Wear on the outskirts of Bishop Auckland; dating from 1857, it once carried trains to Durham. When viewed in June 1996 the elegant and solid grade II listed structure had been converted to provide for a road. This afforded a considerable improvement to the original road over the nearby medieval bridge. *Author*

BISHOP AUCKLAND and BARNARD CASTLE

Miles		Week Days only							
		Z a.m	**G** a.m	**U**	**L** a.m	**O** a.m		p.m	
—	Bishop Auckland...dep	6 20	9 18	..	9 45	10 0	..	4 12	..
2¾	West Auckland..........	..	..	..	9 52	..	..	4 18	..
5½	Evenwood	..	..	..	9 59	..	..	4 24	..
7¾	Cockfield Fell............	..	..	..	10 6	..	..	4 30	..
15	Barnard Castle.....arr	6 50	9 46	..	10 22	10 30	..	4 45	..

Miles		Week Days only										
		Y a.m	**XE** p.m	**S** p.m		**R** p.m		**T** p.m		**V** p.m		
—	Barnard Castle......dep	8 17	12 4	12 14	..	2 50	..	3 40	..	6 16	..	..
7¾	Cockfield Fell............	8 31	12 18	12 18	..	..	..	..				
9½	Evenwood	8 36	12 23	12 23	..							
12¼	West Auckland..........	8 41	12 28	12 28	..							
15	Bishop Auckland...arr	8 47	12 34	12 34	..	3 16	..	4 4	..	6 43	..	..

E Except Saturdays.
G Saturdays only. Runs 2nd July to 20th August. Through Train to Blackpool (N.) arr 1 40 pm (Table 55).
L Saturdays only. Not after 3rd September. Through Train to Blackpool (Cen.) arr 2 24 pm (Table 55).
O Through Train from Durham (Table 59).

R Saturdays only. Runs 9th July to 27th August. Through Train from Blackpool (N.) dep 11 5 am to South Shields arr 4 55 pm (Tables 55, 59 and 69).
S Saturdays only
T Saturdays only. Runs 25th June to 10th Sept. Through Train Blackpool (Cen.) dep 11 20 am to Newcastle (Tables 55 and 59).
I Through Train from Middleton-in-Teesdale (Table 58).

U Through Train from Sunderland (Table 59).
V Through Train Middleton-in-Teesdale to Sunderland (Tables 58 and 59).
X Through Train Middleton-in-Teesdale and Durham (Tables 58 and 59).
Y Through Train Middleton-in-Teesdale to Sunderland (to South Shields arr 10 43 am 25th July to 3rd September) (Tables 58, 59 and 69).
Z Through Train from Newcastle (Tables 67 and 59).

Top: Timetable for Bishop Auckland and Barnard Castle services, July 1955.

Above: Willington station on the Bishop Auckland-Durham line, with a train to Bishop Auckland waiting at the gas-lit platform on 1 May 1962. Passenger services ended two years later. *I. S. Carr*

L.N.E.R. PRIVILEGE
WILLINGTON to BRANDON COLLIERY
SPECIMEN
WILLINGTON to BRANDON COLLIERY
Available within one ... of date of issue

L.N.E.R. For conditions see back — Available for three days including day of issue — Bishop Auckland to ETHERLEY OR HUNWICK — ETHERLEY etc — 3rd 6d 2

NORTH EASTERN RAILWAY.
Spennymoor
From YORK

Above: Gas-lit Brandon Colliery station on the Bishop Auckland-Durham line on 30 April 1962. Steps led down to the platform from the smoke-stained wooden booking office, although a steep ramp also gave access from the road. *I. S. Carr*

Below: Spennymoor station on 8 November 1952 with Class A5/2 4-6-2 No 69835. Passenger services to Bishop Auckland ended in December 1939 and to Ferryhill in March 1952. However, passenger excursions continued to run until the line's closure to freight in the mid-1960s. *W. Armstrong*

Leamside and the lost main line

A banquet held at Newcastle Central station in 1850 celebrated the completion of the ECML from London to Scotland. The route at that time was somewhat different from today, as were the trains that used it. The ECML has witnessed much change. The last regular steam train used the line in 1965 and the last 'Deltic' in 1982. The 1970s saw the introduction of the High Speed Train and the electrified service was launched in the 1990s.

This was one route that even Dr Beeching had to concede might just be worth retaining, at least south of Newcastle. Parts are closed or 'mothballed' (out of use, but kept *in situ* for possible future use), not because the route has become a lost line, but because alternative lines were made available, or improvements to the old route have been made. The most substantial section to be mothballed was the 19-mile (30.6km) section that ran from Tursdale Junction at Ferryhill, via Leamside, to Pelaw Junction. The route was known as the old main line, or in later years as the Leamside line.

The Leamside line did not develop in a planned way, but emerged from a number of short individual routes that were connected to provide a main line. The stretch south from Washington, via Rainton Crossing, to Rainton Meadows near Leamside, opened in August 1838 and was the first section to be used by passenger trains in March 1840. Services were operated by the Durham Junction Railway, but in 1844 this became part of the Newcastle & Darlington Junction Railway (N&DJR), with wider ambitions of running between the towns named in its title. A section north from Washington, via Brockley Whins to Pelaw, combined with two sections south, from Rainton Crossing to Shincliffe and to Ferryhill, were all opened to passenger traffic by the N&DJR in June 1844.

In October 1850 a more direct route between Washington and Pelaw via Usworth, which had opened to freight the previous year, was used by passenger trains. Collectively, the sections between Ferryhill and Pelaw acted as part of the ECML between Darlington and Newcastle.

The largest engineering work on the line was the Victoria Bridge, which was so named because of its completion close to Queen Victoria's coronation in 1838. The viaduct has 10 arches and the 160ft (49m) central span stands at over 130ft (40m) above the River Wear. The design was based on a Roman bridge at Alcántara in Spain.

In 1872 a new line to Newcastle via Durham was opened and this soon became the main ECML. The Leamside line remained as an alternative route and the first significant passenger closure was not until the local Ferryhill-Leamside passenger service ceased in July 1941, while the substantial Leamside station

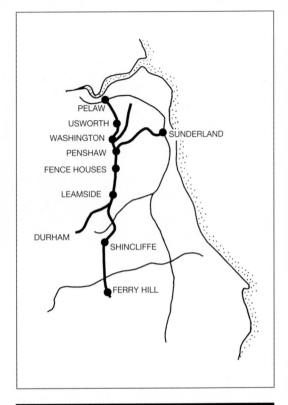

Below: Penshaw North: a view from the footplate of NCB 0-6-2T No 31 with a coal train from Penshaw yard for the staithes at Sunderland. This NCB line adjacent to Penshaw North box joined the BR Penshaw North-Sunderland line at Cox Green Junction, the NCB trains having running powers over BR metals. This view was taken on 9 June 1965; the NCB workings ceased in January 1967 and the BR line itself was closed between Penshaw North and Hylton in August 1967. *I. S. Carr*

Right: Class V3 No 67688 at Penshaw with an up parcels train. This was one of the few jobs left for these engines, together with empty stock and pilot duties, at the time when this photograph was taken on 5 September 1960. *C. Walker*

Below: Sulzer Type 2 No D5148 passes Penshaw North with an up freight on the Leamside line on 26 August 1964. The line to Hylton and Sunderland, which closed to passengers in 1964 and to freight three years later, diverges to the right beyond the signalbox. The ex-NCB line to Cox Green Junction was formerly at the foot of the retaining wall on the right. *I. S. Carr*

closed in October 1953. However, the Leamside line, together with the links to Durham and Sunderland, were all identified for closure in the Beeching Report. The remaining passenger services between Pelaw and Fencehouses, together with the link between Durham and Sunderland, ended in May 1964, although some stations reopened for one day in the following July for the Durham Miners' Gala.

The Leamside line was used extensively for freight traffic, including coal from nearby workings. At Washington, iron ore trains would at one time be marshalled for the haul up to Consett steelworks. The line was also frequently used as a diversionary route for the ECML, but was last used during the electrification of the ECML and closed to all through traffic in 1991.

The line was subsequently mothballed, rather than closed, because of the possibility of future use in connection with open-cast coal workings in the area; indeed, the Pelaw-Wardley section remains in use for this purpose. Elsewhere, since mothballing much contraction has taken place; the line was singled and signalboxes at Usworth, Fencehouses and Whitwell were demolished in 1995. With the exception of the Pelaw-Wardley section, where once the greatest trains in the land thundered, currently all is silent.

Left: After a temporary period of closure for engineering works, the Leamside line was reopened in the summer of 1979 for diversions to the ECML. Diverted via the Leamside line on Sunday 1 November 1981, the 11.25 Edinburgh-Plymouth train comes off the single track section from Washington at Penshaw North behind Class 47 No 47557. The signalbox just about survives. *I. S. Carr*

Below: Class 37 No 37036 and brake van to the exchange sidings on the NCB Philadelphia system seen at Penshaw North on 13 September 1982. Note that the signalbox has been demolished. *L. Abram*

Right: English Electric Type 4 No D382 heads the up 'Highlands Car Sleeper' Inverness-York train over the Victoria Bridge, between Washington and Penshaw, at 6.14am on 26 June 1966. The train had been diverted because of engineering work on the ECML. The bridge, which dates from 1838, was based on the design of a Roman bridge at Alcántara in Spain. *I. S. Carr*

Bottom: A three-car DMU on the 'Rail 150 Tour' from Darlington. The train was run in connection with the 150th anniversary of the S&DR. The tour is seen here passing Washington (the ancestral home of George Washington) on Saturday 19 July 1975. *I. S. Carr*

North Eastern Railway

From————————

Fencehouses

NORTH EASTERN RAILWAY.

From YORK.

LEAMSIDE

Left: Class 45 No 45006 on the 12.25 Newcastle train, diverted via Leamside, on Sunday 2 May 1982. The remains of the South Pelaw line can be seen next to the signal post; note that Washington signalbox has been vandalised since closure. *L. Abram*

Centre left: Against a background of open-cast coal mining, Class 47 No 47552 was photographed on Sunday 15 March 1987 at Leamside with the 10.00 Newcastle-Penzance train, diverted because of engineering work on the ECML. There is today no trace of the once substantial Leamside station. *I. S. Carr*

Below: The 'mothballed' and single rusting Leamside line at Shincliffe station, which was being used as a restaurant when this view was taken in July 1996. *Author*

NORTH EASTERN RAILWAY

From YORK.

PENSHAW

17 Closures to Consett

In the 1850s abundant supplies of iron ore were found in the Cleveland Hills. There was excellent coking coal in south Durham and limestone — which is used as a flux in steel making — could be obtained at Stanhope in the Pennines. The coast facilitated exports and shipyards flourished, using immense quantities of iron and steel. As a result Consett's great iron industry developed. The works at Consett, on the Durham moorland, were about 800ft (244m) above sea level. In later years, when iron ore was imported, difficulties were created in that the steep gradients to Consett required many trains to be assisted by banking engines.

The Stanhope & Tyne Railroad was the first line to serve Consett, opening from Stanhope via Rowley to Consett in May 1834 and running eastward to the coast, near Tyne Dock, by September of the same year. The line went bankrupt and the western section was sold to the Derwent Iron Company at Consett. The S&DR looked to expand into the area and the iron company agreed to sell its part of the line to the railway in return for a new link to that system. The connecting line to Crook opened to freight in May 1845, becoming known as the Wear & Derwent Junction Railway, a subsidiary of the S&DR. Passenger services ran from nearby Blackhill (for a time this station was also known as Consett) some 15.5 miles (25km) to Crook in September 1845.

In 1858, at Hownsgill between Consett and Rowley, the S&DR replaced inclines on the existing line by a viaduct. The 12 elegant yellow firebrick arches of the viaduct extended some 729ft (222m) in length and up to 150ft (46m) in height. The structure was designed by Sir Thomas Bouch. Consequently buttresses were added to the structure after his Tay Bridge collapsed. Happily, when much other evidence of the line has gone, Hownsgill Viaduct still stands.

By the 1860s the Consett ironworks complex was soundly established and a second line opened from Blackhill, via the Lanchester Valley, to Durham in September 1862. In December 1867 a further route was opened, via the Derwent Valley, to Scotswood west of Newcastle. Together the lines formed a loop via Blackhill between Durham and Newcastle. The ironworks and collieries in the area soon provided considerable freight traffic and the loop was doubled for much of its length.

Right: In June 1964 Class Q6 0-8-0 No 63409 approaches Consett on a coal train with another 'Q6' banking. Extensive sidings store NCB trucks. *W. J. V. Anderson*

The main passenger flow was to Tyneside and numbers increased steadily until World War 1. After this, the general decline in the area's industry, bus competition and the fact that a number of stations were not conveniently located, significantly reduced passenger traffic. The first major closure came when the Blackhill-Tow Law passenger services were suspended in May 1939, together with the service via Lanchester to Durham at the same time. Passenger services via the Derwent Valley to Blackhill closed in February 1954, ending a further loop line service back to Newcastle via Consett and Beamish. The final passenger service from Blackhill to Newcastle, via Consett and Beamish, ended in May 1955.

Freight remained longer, but the decline of the Consett works and the shutting of collieries resulted in the eventual closure of all freight lines in the area. The Derwent Valley line closed to freight in November 1963 and the Lanchester Valley line in June 1966. After several cutbacks, the final stretch of the line from Consett towards Stanhope, to a munitions depot at Burnhill, closed in May 1969.

The last remaining freight line to Consett was a section of the old Stanhope and Tyne line running east to the Leamside line at Washington. After closure of the steelworks in 1980 the massive structures were demolished and the scrap transported on this route, together with a few weekly wagonloads of domestic coal. In March 1983 the link to Blackhill coal yard closed and after 150 years of rail service the official last train to Consett ran in March 1984.

With the steelworks site levelled and landscaped, a railway truck that once carried molten metal, together with a number of bridges and earthworks are all that remain in the Consett area. Nearby Rowley station, which I noted in my diary in 1965 as being very run-down, was moved stone by stone to the Beamish Museum. Finally, Consett is now the focus of a network of footpaths, the Waskerley Way, Derwent Walk, Lanchester Valley Walk and the Consett and Sunderland Railway Path, all using the lost lines to the town.

Below: Map of the Consett area in 1923. *Crown Copyright*

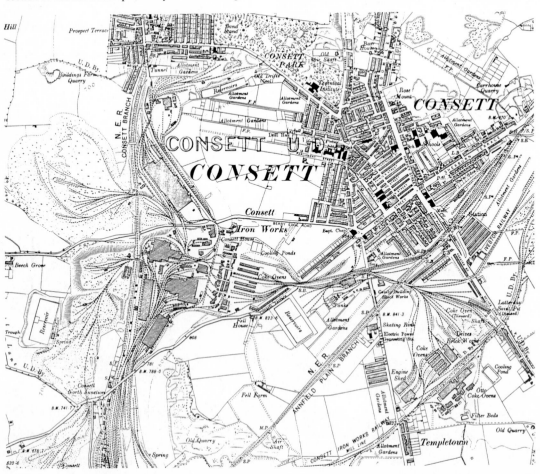

Left: Class Q6 0-8-0 No 63346 shunts at South Pelaw after working a heavy coal train. Here No 63346 will split the train before tackling the climb to Consett with eight 21-ton hoppers — the maximum for a 'Q6' without a banker. *V. Wake*

Above: BR Standard Class 9F 2-10-0 No 92099 storms the climb to Pelton with a Tyne Dock-Consett iron ore train; '9F' No 92066 is the banking engine on 8 April 1964. Not only was this action being captured on film, someone was also making a sound recording of this impressive event. *D. Hardy*

Below: Having divided the train from Stella Gill sidings into two, BR Standard Class 9F 2-10-0 No 92062 leaves South Pelaw, accompanied by much smoke and steam, with a coal train for Consett in November 1964. *W. J. V. Anderson*

Left: BR Standard Class 9F 2-10-0 No 92097 at Tyne Dock with an iron ore train for Consett in November 1963. The last steam-hauled train — pulled by a '9F' — ran to Consett three years later. *R. Kell*

Below: Consett Low Yard on 5 August 1969 with the increasingly dilapidated works seen in the background. Two English Electric Type 3s, No 6712 as pilot to No 6791, prepare to depart with the 20.35 Consett-Cargo Fleet 'molten metal' train. *J. M. Boyes*

Right: On 17 March 1984 Class 46 No 46026 *Leicestershire and Derbyshire Yeomanry* awaits departure from Consett for Newcastle, the last official train. The headboard incorporates the smokebox numberplate from No 92066, one of the '9F' steam locomotives that once worked the Tyne Dock-Consett iron ore trains. *I. S. Carr*

Above: Low Yard at Consett North on 22 December 1981. An effort is being made to remove a snowdrift with a mechanical digger, but there is not much other activity. *L. Abram*

Right: Low Yard at Consett North on 15 August 1984 with track lifting in progress; the signalbox has already been demolished and the desolation of the site is evident from this view. Continuous welded rail and concrete sleepers recovered from remaining routes to the yard were reused elsewhere in the northeast, including on the Whitby line. *L. Abram*

Above: Hownsgill Viaduct, south of Consett, in July 1996. Designed by Thomas Bouch and completed by 1858, the viaduct's graceful spans stretch for almost 730ft (222m) and reach 150ft (46m) at their tallest. *Author*

Left: Coming off Hownsgill Viaduct and heading for Consett in July 1996. Deepest countryside, cyclists and pedestrians have replaced the once vast industrial areas and iron and coal trains. *Author*

Below left: A souvenir of the steelworks. This wagon once conveyed molten metal around the vast works area. It now lies in a park as a reminder of Consett's industrial past. *Author*

Right: The Port of Blyth on 15 July 1965: 'Q6' 0-8-0 No 63386 makes a fine show as it storms out from the coal staithes. Scrapping of these ex-NER Raven-designed engines began in 1960. The staithes were demolished by the early part of 1996 to provide a larger turning circle for ships. Conveyors are now used to export coal from the port. *Ian Allan Library*

18 The twilight trains

In the northeast hundreds of pits have been closed and 1994 saw the last miners 'gannin doon the pit' at Easington in Durham. The business of coal mining was dominated by rail transport, which itself was fuelled by coal, and millions of tons of coal were once all conveyed by rail. A huge fleet of steam locomotives was used for this and other freight work in the area.

The locomotives needed constant care, which in turn resulted in a well-known feature of the railway: the steam locomotive shed. The sheds provided more than just protection from the weather — they supplied coal, water, servicing and repairs to those steam locomotives 'on shed'. They often covered substantial areas and although some sheds were later adapted for use by diesel locomotives, with the demise of steam, most steam sheds were closed and subsequently demolished.

It was clear even in the 1960s that a whole way of life was rapidly disappearing. Rail freight was in serious decline in the northeast, which, together with a policy of diesel replacement, resulted in a growing surplus of steam motive power. Yet whilst relatively modern steam engines could be observed awaiting scrap, some of the most reliable classes of freight locomotives, dating back to the NER, could still be seen working. The old machines were revered by many and some 'shed-bashers' secretly polished the old engines up by night, not only to get good photographs, but also as a last act of kindness to the languishing locomotives.

During the twilight of steam, most of the staff who operated the locomotive sheds were ambassadors for BR. They had to ensure a fine balance was struck between the safe running of their shed and not disappointing enthusiasts, who would have such a limited opportunity to record the last days of steam. Visitors were not encouraged, but many shed staff recognised the uniqueness of this sunset of steam and turned a blind eye to the enthusiasts.

My diary records an interesting week in the school holidays:

Wednesday, 9 August 1967; Went to Sunderland, it was a very wet day, but there was an excellent selection of locomotives on shed. I felt a bit of a criminal rushing about between the engines to take photographs. I asked a man if it was all

right to photograph, but he said, 'Don't ask, just take what you want and quickly go.'

Sunday, 13 August 1967; This was the chance of a lifetime! The Shed Master at West Hartlepool said we could photograph what we wanted and let us put our bags in his office so we could take better photographs. I was even offered a ride on one of the engines, WD Austerity 2-8-0 No 90074. I drove it backwards and managed to get stuck in a dip in the rails. I opened the regulator, but the engine would not move as there was not much steam left. Finally, I took the plunge, aided and abetted by the driver, opening the regulator really wide. The engine lurched forward and with a terrific thump hit the wagons and 'chopped' them, so they said. Anyway they stayed on the rails even if they did look a bit crooked.

Steam disappeared from the northeast the following month, in September 1967. Both Hartlepool and Sunderland sheds have since disappeared, together with all the activity that went with them. But fond memories live on.

Below: Dirty and run-down, 'J27' 0-6-0 No 65874 negotiates the level crossing at Bedlington with a coal train on 18 July 1966. Scrapping of this class commenced in 1959, but the hard working engines lasted to the end of steam in the northeast. *C. Kenyon*

Above: Class Q6 0-8-0 No 63354 clanks through Ashington station with a coal train from Newbiggin-by-the-Sea on 22 October 1964. Passenger services ceased from Ashington the following month. *M. Dunnett*

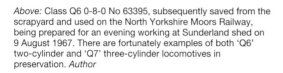

Above: Class Q6 0-8-0 No 63395, subsequently saved from the scrapyard and used on the North Yorkshire Moors Railway, being prepared for an evening working at Sunderland shed on 9 August 1967. There are fortunately examples of both 'Q6' two-cylinder and 'Q7' three-cylinder locomotives in preservation. *Author*

Above: A 'Q6' class 0-8-0, shorn of its numberplate, standing forlornly out of use and waiting to be scrapped on a wet day at Sunderland shed on 9 August 1967. *Author*

Above: Class Q6 No 63407 out of use at West Hartlepool on 13 August 1967. BR inherited all 120 of these successful locomotives. Built between 1913 and 1918 for hauling trains of

1,500 tons, scrapping began only after 50 years of service, and the engines became some of the last to work in the northeast. *Author*

Left: Class Q6 0-8-0 No 63421 — a view taken from on top of the tender! The engine was out of use, awaiting scrap at West Hartlepool on 13 August 1967. *Author*

Below: No 63431 minus its coupling rods and waiting to be scrapped at West Hartlepool on 13 August 1967. The ruggedness and reliability of Sir Vincent Raven's design gave these ex-NER freight locomotives a remarkable longevity; they outlived many of the later BR Standard classes. *Author*

Below: WD 2-8-0 No 90074 at West Hartlepool on 13 August 1967. This class was designed by R. A. Riddles to meet wartime requirements, and No 90074 was built in 1944. It was withdrawn in September 1967, but not before it had been 'driven' a very short way by the author when he was a schoolboy. *Author*

19 Newcastle Quayside

The Northumberland and Durham coalfield covered an area from the Cheviot Hills and Pennines to the coast, from the River Coquet in the north to Hartlepool in the south. At the centre of this area and at the lowest bridging point on the River Tyne, the fine industrial city of Newcastle upon Tyne developed as the most important coal-shipping centre in the country. Railways were 'to take coals to Newcastle' and from the 1840s onwards the Tyne was a particularly active and important river.

Historically the use of Newcastle Quayside dates back many centuries, but in June 1870 the NER opened a line to the quayside. Tunnels formed a 0.75-mile (1.2km) spiral that descended the Tyne gorge, from near Manors station to the north bank of the river, close to the heart of the city. The short but steeply graded mineral branch contained gradients as sheer as 1 in 27.

The North Tyne electric services began in 1904 and the system was the first major provincial electrification, just beating the L&YR system at Liverpool. The Quayside branch was not used for passengers, but the short line was connected to the adjacent electrified routes. The decision was taken to include the line in the electrification scheme and electric freight trains ran on the branch from 1905. Unlike the rest of the system, which generally operated with third-rail at 600V dc, the freight branch was electrified with a mix of third-rail and overhead catenary. The overhead catenary was to obviate the dangers of freight loading with ground level electric rails in the yards at each end of the branch. However, in the restricted tunnels third-rail was used.

The two electric freight locomotives provided for the route were equipped with overhead pantographs in addition to third-rail pick-up shoes. The steeple-cab Bo-Bo electric locomotives were built by British Thomson Houston and looked remarkably modern in design. They were also highly successful and were to outlive other electric stock of the period. The 10 electric freight locomotives on the Shildon-Newport

Below: In contrast to the tranquillity of its remote rural expanses, the region also embraced the roar of great industrial areas. This photograph was taken at Newcastle in December 1983, looking north, and shows roof demolition and infilling of Platforms 1, 2 and 3. The North Tyneside electrification was completed in 1904 and between 1917 and 1967 electric trains used these platforms for services to the coast. *I. S. Carr*

line ceased work in 1934 and were subsequently scrapped, while in 1937 new red and cream all-steel electric passenger stock replaced the older NER electric cars on Tyneside.

In 1962 Dr Beeching stunned a northern industrialists' luncheon with the warning that losses on the Tyneside electric services might result in their closure. Most lines survived, but by 1967 electric services had been replaced by diesel operation. In 1964 diesel locomotives replaced the electric ones on the Quayside branch. However, with the decline of the upper Tyne river trade in the 1960s, the Quayside freight route was closed in June 1969.

The quayside has since formed an important part of Newcastle's refurbished riverside, but some traces of the branch and the tunnels still remain. Furthermore, NER No 1, a Bo-Bo electric locomotive dating from 1902 and used on the line, is preserved at the NRM.

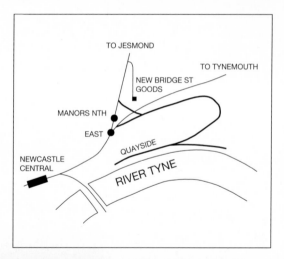

Left: Ex-NER Class ES1 Bo-Bo electric locomotive No 26501 shunting beside the River Tyne on the cobbled Newcastle quayside. Haulage on the branch was chiefly done by the two 600V dc electric locomotives of this type. Note the single electric headlamp. Shunting on the quayside was mainly carried out by steam engines. *J. D. Smith*

Below left: The semicircular tunnel that led from the quayside up to Manors station still survived in July 1996 when this view of the west-facing quayside portal was taken. The quayside itself has been extensively redeveloped and little else remains of this branch on the Tyne riverside. *Author*

Above right: Two NER engines built almost 50 years apart — electric locomotive Class ES1 No 26500 dating from 1902 in front of 'J72' 0-6-0 No 69024 dating from 1951 — standing at New Bridge Street at Newcastle in February 1962. *R. G. Warwick*

Right: This photograph shows the same scene as that in the previous photograph but was taken in 1996 near Manors station. Note the reversal of fortunes, with the quayside branch catenary removed and the former third-rail lines now electrified with overhead wires. *Author*

Left: Electric locomotive No 26500 in NER green livery at Trafalgar Yard, after making its last trip from the quayside on 29 February 1964. From this date the line was worked by diesel shunters until its eventual closure in 1969. Note the changeover from third-rail pick-up through tunnels to overhead wire in the yards. *I. S. Carr*

Centre left: Electric locomotive No 26501 stands forlornly in the rain at Choppington, Northumberland, on 7 August 1966. The locomotive, which had previously been stored at Hellifield, was cut up later in the week. *I. S. Carr*

Bottom left: Bo-Bo electric locomotive No 26500 met a kinder fate and was preserved as part of the National Railway Collection. It is seen here outside the NRM at York. *Courtesy NRM*

Right: A September 1971 view of the tangerine hand-painted Haltwhistle nameboard, the signalbox, footbridge and gas-lit Alston branch platform, which is to the right of this view. *A. Muckley*

The 13-mile (21km) line that ran from Haltwhistle to Alston was opened in November 1852 by the Newcastle & Carlisle Railway. It was a charming branch line which ran from the main line at Haltwhistle into the northern Pennines and to Alston, one of the highest market towns in England. The route used the deep and narrowing river valley of the South Tyne to the east of Cold Fell and Three Pikes, but plans for a further extension into Weardale never came to fruition.

In negotiating the valley of the South Tyne the line embraced a number of attractive viaducts of various sizes, all of which remain. Designed by Sir George Barclay-Bruce, that at Lambley is slender and curving, while at Burnstones, near Slaggyford, the viaduct is skewed in one way or another. A solid looking viaduct crosses the waters of the South Tyne near Haltwhistle. Many stations on the line were equally well built, mainly in stone, to an appealing form of Tudor design.

In harsh winter weather the line was a lifeline, as the shelter of the river valley allowed the railway to operate on some occasions when the road was impassable. Lead was mined on Alston Moor and mineral freight, including coal from Lambley, used the branch. Indeed freight was important on the line until well after World War 2, but passenger services were always more limited and there was no Sunday service.

DMUs were introduced in 1959, but the line was identified in the Beeching Report for closure and by 1965 freight had ended. However, attempts to end passenger services on the line were thwarted because of its remoteness and the severe winter weather that can affect this area of the high northern Pennines. Economies were made and a basic pay train service continued, but trains on the branch involved a change at Haltwhistle and a new 'all-weather' road was promised. After a fight the branch was eventually closed in May 1976.

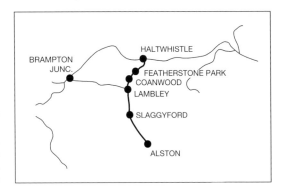

My diary describes a trip on the line:

Wednesday, 9 August 1967; Went to Haltwhistle via North Wylam. The line to Alston is beautiful and typically branch-like. On the return trip the guard let a regular passenger off the train at his factory, the driver was none too pleased as there was no station. I asked for a ticket to Slaggyford. The guard gave me an ordinary green bus ticket which was just about useless for my collection! We eventually returned to the Youth Hostel at Carlisle, which was next to Kingmoor shed, and went to sleep to the sound of steam engines.

Above: A DMU crosses the solid stone six-arched viaduct over the River South Tyne and climbs away from Haltwhistle with the 15.34 to Alston on 26 August 1970. *I. S. Carr*

After closure there were immediate attempts to preserve the line, but the track was lifted. In 1980 agreement was reached to construct a narrow gauge line north from Alston and the first mile opened in July 1983 as the 2ft (0.6m) South Tynedale Railway. Today there are many narrow gauge locomotives and the line extends back some 2.25 miles (3.6km) to Kirkhaugh. Longer term plans involve a return to Slaggyford and even a reopening of the entire branch.

Left: Lambley station, looking towards Haltwhistle, with a freight train waiting to come off the Lambley colliery line — this line closed in 1960. *N. Stead*

Left: An old NER signal on the Alston branch on 4 September 1971. The lower quadrant signal arm went into a slot in the upper part of the post. The finial at the top of the signal was 4ft (1.2m) in height, its base was cast iron and the uppermost point was made from sheet zinc. *A. Muckley*

Below: Ivatt Class 4 2-6-0 No 43121 has just crossed the slender arches of the 110ft (34m)-high single line Lambley Viaduct with the SLS 'Scottish Rambler Railtour' on Easter Sunday 1967. The viaduct was restored and opened as a public walkway in 1996. *A. Cattle*

Left: Class J39 No 64842 and 'G5' No 67315, an unusual combination, on a two-coach train on the Alston branch in 1950s steam days. In 1956 a journey from King's Cross to Alston took about eight hours and a third class single cost £2 10s 1d. *N. Stead*

Below left: The remote Slaggyford station lies some 4.5 miles (7km) north of Alston; it is seen here with a new nameboard, but still oil-lit, on 4 September 1971. *A. Muckley*

Right: Class J39 0-6-0 No 64812 at Alston station in the early 1950s when the station retained its overall roof and engine shed, although not its turntable. The turntable was originally located in the foreground, below the wall, cleverly avoiding the need for points at the head of the branch. *E. Smith*

Centre right: The overall station roof at Alston survived until about 1967, although it was stripped of its wooden ends. The engine shed, which closed in 1959 when DMUs were introduced, had already lost its roof when this photograph was taken. *Ian Allan Library*

Below right: The handsome stone exterior of Alston station. Dating from 1852 and serving one of the highest market towns in England, it is viewed here from the gas-lit approach on 4 September 1971. *A. Muckley*

Table 73   HALTWHISTLE and ALSTON

Miles from Haltwhistle	Week Days only											
		a.m	a.m	..	a.m	a.m	..	p.m	p.m	p.m	p m	p.m	..
			S		S	E		S	E	S		S	
	70 Newcastle dep	6 40	8 20	..	10 30	1030	..	1220	4 20	6 20	6 20	8 20	..
	70 Carlisle "	6 40	8 45	..	10A45	1045	..	1 5	3 55	7 0	7 0	9 5	..
	Haltwhistle... dep	8 0	9 45	..	11 50	12 0	..	1 47	5 40	7 50	8 0	10 5	..
3	Featherstone Park	8 8	9 53	..	11 58	12 8	..	1 55	5 48	7 58	8 8	1013	..
4	Coanwood	8 12	9 57	..	12 2	1212	..	1 59	5 52	8 2	8 12	1017	..
4½	Lambley	8 15	10 0	..	12 5	1215	..	2 2	5 55	8 5	8 15	1020	..
8½	Slaggyford	8 24	10 9	..	12 14	1224	..	2 11	6 4	8 14	8 24	1029	..
13	Alston........ arr	8 35	1020	..	12 25	1235	..	2 22	6 15	8 25	8 35	1040	..

Miles	Week Days only											
		a.m	a.m	..	a.m	p.m	..	p.m	p.m	..	p.m	
			S		S	S						
—	Alston......... dep	7 10	8 55	..	1054	1245	..	4 25	6 50	..	9 0	..	..
4½	Slaggyford	7 20	9 5	..	10 52	1255	..	4 35	7 0	..	9 10	..	..
8½	Lambley	7 29	9 14	..	11 1	1 4	..	4 44	7 9	..	9 19	..	..
9	Coanwood	7 32	9 17	..	11 4	1 7	..	4 47	7 12	..	9 22	..	..
10	Featherstone Park	7 36	9 21	..	11 8	1 11	..	4 51	7 16	..	9 26	..	..
13	Haltwhistle... arr	7 45	9 30	..	11 17	1 20	..	5 0	7 25	..	9 35	..	..
36	70 Carlisle.. arr	8 54	1033	..	12 3	2 24	..	6 11	8 18	..	1040	..	..
50½	70 Newcastle "	9 30	11 2	..	1229	2 57	..	6 37	8 55	..	1115	..	..

A Dep 10 55 am from 25th June to 27th August.   E Except Sats.   F Arr. 12 42 pm on 18th June, 3rd, 10th and 17th September   S Sats. only.

Above: Timetable Haltwhistle and Alston, July 1955.

Left: Alston station on 1 May 1976 with the last train to Haltwhistle on a wet evening and with a special farewell headboard. *A. Muckley*

Below: Alston station is now the headquarters of the narrow gauge South Tynedale Railway. The restored stonework at the attractive terminus building is seen here in December 1982. *Ian Allan Library*

Above: Featherstone Park station, looking towards Haltwhistle in January 1980. In the future it is hoped that trains may well pass through this station once again on their way back to Haltwhistle. *A. Muckley*

Right: An old Pooley weighing machine still survived at the closed Coanwood station in January 1980. Even the smallest of stations included a profusion of fittings that were once a commonplace part of railway operation. *A. Muckley*

21 Alnwick and Alnmouth

The Romans built the Great North Road through Alnwick; later it became an important fortified castle settlement and was once the county town of Northumberland. Sometimes known as the 'Windsor of the North', the town contains many attractive buildings and the White Swan Hotel has a panelled room salvaged from the *Olympic*, the *Titanic's* sister ship, when it was scrapped at Wallsend.

Plans to build the ECML through Alnwick were thwarted by the then Duke of Northumberland. Nevertheless, the need for a rail connection to the town was soon recognised and a 3-mile (5km) branch line between Alnwick and Alnmouth was opened by the York, Newcastle & Berwick Railway in August 1850. The line became part of the NER in 1854. The branch ran in a northwesterly direction from the ECML, broadly following the valley of the River Aln from Alnmouth, which once acted as the port for Alnwick. Alnmouth is where the ECML from London finally reaches the coast, and the town remains a quiet seaside resort with sands and golf facilities.

No intermediate stations were provided on the branch, but at Alnwick a substantial and attractive stone passenger terminus was constructed, with a respectable double overall roof span, designed by William Bell. The new terminus was built by the NER to coincide with the opening of the Cornhill branch in September 1887. This line ran from Alnwick some 35.75 miles (58km) to Coldstream, where connections could once be made to the Waverley route and to Tweedmouth. The Cornhill branch, which ran through a remote area, had a limited service from Alnwick and was one of the first significant stretches of line to close to passengers in September 1930.

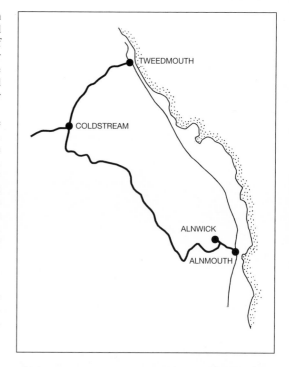

The remaining stump to Alnwick continued rather more successfully. The station was well sited in the town and a relatively frequent shuttle service ran between the terminus and the ECML. Freight traffic was also important, including coal, and the route was not included for closure in the Beeching Report. Unlike some secondary stations in the northeast, electric lights replaced gas on the platforms, but

Left: A 1940s view of Alnwick station's interesting exterior showing the main entrance and station clock. The substantially-built stone terminus was designed by William Bell and dates from 1887. It once provided a regular weekday train service to the ECML and boasted a W. H. Smith shop.
Real Photographs Co

Right: On 12 March 1966 'K1' 2-6-0 No 62011 waiting to depart with a two-coach Alnwick-Alnmouth train. The interior of the station was spacious, light and well protected from the elements. *J. Boyes*

DMUs were not introduced until 1966, making this one of the last steam-operated branches in the country. Nevertheless, in the 1960s the retention of such rural branches appeared to be an anathema. Through trains to Newcastle had been reduced over the years and, despite strong local objections, the line was closed to passengers in January 1968 and to freight in October of the same year.

After closure, a freight shed at Alnwick was moved to the Beamish Museum, but the main passenger terminus was spared from demolition and was used by an agricultural merchant. Plans to reopen the line have received much support, including that from the present Duke of Northumberland. Although two new bridges would be required, much of the trackbed endures, together with the interchange platform at Alnmouth. The main stone-built passenger terminus at Alnwick remains in good order, parts have been restored to the original condition and the building already houses a railway museum.

Right: On 18 June 1966 the same engine as in the picture below, No 62011, waits at Alnwick prior to departing with the 12.45 train to Alnmouth. *P. K. King*

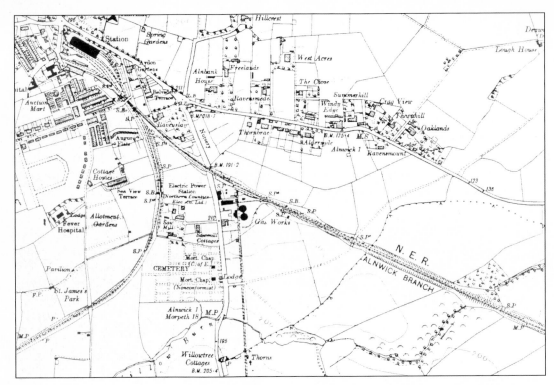

Miles		a.m	a.m	a.m	a.m		E	S	a.m		N	G		C	Z S	S		p.m	Z	E		S	E	p.m	S		p.m	Z	
	Alnmouth .... dep	6 30	7 43	8 30	9 0	..	9 50	9 56	10 25	..	12 30	1 19	..	1 34	1 47	1 58	..	5 22	6 10	7 14	..	7 35	8 0	8 35	8 36	..	10 17	11 52	..
	Alnwick .... arr	6 37	7 50	8 37	9 7	..	9 57	10 3	10 32	..	12 37	1 29	..	1 41	1 54	2 5	..	5 29	6 17	7 21	..	7 42	8 7	8 42	9 43	..	10 24	11 59	..

Week Days only

Miles		a.m	Z	a.m		a.m	Z S		a.m	N		p.m	S	Z		S	E	E		S	E	p.m		S		p.m	p.m	
	Alnwick .... dep	7 10	7 27	8 17	8 44	..	9 32	10 0	..	10 8	12 14	..	12 50	1 40	4 25	..	4 52	5 0	6 58	..	7 16	7 45	8 20	..	9 14	..	9 58	11 0	..
3	Alnmouth .... arr	7 16	7 33	8 23	8 50	..	9 38	10 6	..	10 14	12 20	..	12 56	1 46	4 31	..	4 58	5 6	7 4	..	7 22	7 51	8 26	..	9 20	..	10 4	11 6	..

C Tuesdays and Thursdays only. Runs 5th July to 25th August
E Except Saturdays
F 2 minutes later on Saturdays
G Except Tuesdays and Thursdays, 5th July to 25th August
N Saturdays only. Runs 2nd July to 3rd September
S Saturdays only
Z Through Train from or to Newcastle (Table 3)

Left: Alnwick station area in 1926. *Crown Copyright*

Below left: Class K1 2-6-0 No 62012 runs round its train at the appealing terminus at Alnwick on 27 June 1964. Steam drifts behind the lovely collection of former NER signals. *M. Dunnett*

Above: Alnmouth and Alnwick timetable, 1955.

Right: A train to Alnmouth at Alnwick on 5 April 1966, with 'K1' 2-6-0 No 62050. The 'K1' engines were strong and reliable, but with the transition from steam to diesel, they started to be taken out of service from 1962. *D. Bosomworth*

Below: Class K1 2-6-0 No 62011 shunts at Alnwick on 18 June 1966 between passenger duties. This was the last day of steam on the branch and the burnished locomotive was looking particularly smart. *V. Wake*

Above: The platform electric lights were removed once two-car DMUs mainly used the converted part of the terminal at Alnwick, viewed on a wet August day in 1967. The flower beds are empty and the line closed in January of the following year. *Author*

Below: On 14 May 1966 'K1' No 62021 climbs the 1 in 77 grade through woodland towards Alnwick on the 16.48 from Alnmouth. The rising gradients from Alnmouth resulted in the journey to Alnwick taking seven minutes, but the time allocated to the easier descending return trip was six minutes. *M. Burn*

Left: The preserved station clock at Alnwick in October 1996. A nearby window details the names of the seven stationmasters in charge of the terminus from 1887 to 1968. *Author*

Right: The main entrance to Alnwick station remains almost entirely in its original condition, as this view taken in October 1996 shows. *Author*

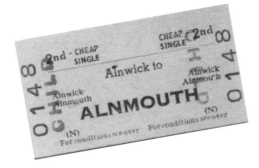

Below: A 1996 view looking along the northern flank of the stone-built and not inconsiderable Alnwick station. The first locomotive arrived on the site in October 1996 as the momentum grew for the reopening of the branch. *Author*

22 The Border Counties Railway

The countryside in this most northerly part of England remains wild, uncompromising and remote. The incentives for the construction of a railway in this area were therefore to draw upon coal reserves at Plashetts, high in the Northumberland hills and to gain access to Tyneside. The single line generally followed the river valley of the North Tyne and joined the Waverley route at the renowned Riccarton Junction. Opening from Hexham to Chollerford in April 1858, the line was completed, via Plashetts and Kielder, to Riccarton Junction by July 1862. At Reedsmouth the route divided, with a line running east along the Wansbeck valley to Morpeth.

The meandering route followed natural features wherever possible but involved some engineering works, such as the castellated Kielder Viaduct built to match Kielder Castle on the instructions of the Duke of Northumberland. It is generally acknowledged that the viaduct is the first and finest surviving example of a particularly complex geometrical skew arch form of construction.

As it turned out, the coal reserves at Plashetts were of poor quality and the Border Counties Railway ran into financial difficulties. The line was soon taken over by the North British Railway, which had the advantage of being able to run services from Hexham into Newcastle as a concession for not thwarting the NER's takeover of the Newcastle & Carlisle Railway.

The route achieved some notoriety in that the locomotive involved in the 1879 Tay Bridge disaster,

Left: Class J21 0-6-0 No 65033 heads a one-coach Hexham-Kielder train north of Wall station, which itself was shut before the rest of this line closed to passengers in 1956. The locomotive was later preserved. *N. Stead*

Below: Timetable for July 1955 showing the limited stopping service.

Right: Humshaugh station with 'J21' No 65033 and a train for Hexham from Riccarton Junction in BR days. Note the attractive station gardens and beehives. Special trains were run in the 1950s to view station gardens on the line, but those at Humshaugh became overgrown before the line was finally removed. After closure of the line the station buildings were restored and put to new uses. *J. W. Armstrong*

Table 80 HEXHAM and RICCARTON JUNCTION (Week Days only

Miles		a.m A	a.m S		a.m B	p.m B	p.m S	Miles		a.m B	a.m A	p.m S		p.m B		A Through Trains between Newcastle and Riccarton Junction
	70 NEWCASTLE 71 .. dep	5 52	9 45		11 10	4 27	8 20		EDINBURGH(W.). dep	..	6 38	..		2 33		B Through Trains between Newcastle and Hawick
—	Hexham .... dep	6 58	1039		12 6	5 16	9 15		HAWICK .. 71	6 15	8 53	..		4 32		8 3 minutes later on Saturdays
3½	Wall..................	7 7	..		12 15	5 25	..	—	Riccarton Junc.... dep	6 47	10 22	..		5 13		F 2 minutes later on Saturdays
5	Humshaugh	7 12	1050		12 20	5 50	..	5½	Deadwater.............	Kk	10 32	..		5 19		J Passengers can arr. at 12 44 p.m. by changing at Hexham
6½	Chollerton	7 17	1054		12 24	5 34	..	8½	Kielder Forest.........	7 3	10 38	..	1 40	5 24		K Arr. 2 20 p.m. on Mons. and Thurs., and 2 22 p.m. on Sats.
7½	Barrasford.........	7 21	..		12 28	5 38	9 34	10	Lewiefield Halt.........	7 8	10 43	..	1 46	5 28		
11½	Wark...............	7 30	11 4		12 36	5 46	9 42	11½	Plashetts.............	7 11	10 47	..	1 51	5 36		Kk Calls at 6 55 a.m. when required to take up on informing the Station Master at Riccarton Junc. before 5 0 p.m. the day previous to travel
15½	Reedsmouth... {arr	7 38	1112		12 44	5 54	9 50	16½	Thorneyburn.........	7 15	..	2 0	2 7	5 43		
	{dep	7 46	1119		12 48	6 1	9 55	20½	Thorneyburn.........	7 27	11 3	2 8				S Saturdays only
17	Bellingham (NorthTyne)	7 51	1124		12 53	6 7	10 0	21½	Tarset...............	7 31	11 7	2 11		5 48		U Arr. 1 53 p.m. Mondays, Thursdays and Saturdays
20½	Tarset............	7 58	1131		1 0	6 13	10 5	25	Bellingham (NorthTyne)	7 38	11 14	2 18		5 55		
21½	Thorneyburn.........	8 2	1135		1 4	6 17	1010	26½	Reedsmouth......{ arr	7 42	11 18	2 22		5 59		Z Passengers can arr. 7 21 p.m. by changing at Hexham
25½	Falstone...........	8 10	1143		1 13	6 25	1018		{ dep	7 48	11 21	2 25		6 4		
30½	Plashetts..........	8 20	1158		1 23	6 35	1028	30½	Wark................	7 57	11 30	2 35		6 13		‡ 4 mins. later on Saturdays
32	Lewiefield Halt	8 26	1158		1 28	6 40	1033	34½	Barrasford..........	8 4	11 37	2 42		6 20		
33½	Kielder Forest......	8 34	12 5		1 35	6 47	1041	35½	Chollerton..........	8 8	11 41	2 46		6 24		
36½	Deadwater.........	8 40	..		1 41	..	..	37	Humshaugh.........	8 13	11 45	2 50		6 28		
42	Riccarton Junc.... arr	8 50	..		1051	7 2	..	38½	Wall...............	8 18	11 49	2 54		6 32		
								42	Hexham............ arr	8 27	11 58	3 3		6 41		
55	HAWICK......... arr	1044	..		2 17	7 27	..	62½	70 NEWCASTLE 71 arr	9 7	1 10	..	3 48	8 7		
107¾	EDINBURGH(Way) .. arr	1220	..		4 24	10 25	..									

118

after spending almost four months in the Firth of Tay, was recovered, repaired and used for some years on this line. NBR 4-4-0 No 224 was nicknamed 'Dipper' and lasted until 1919. In the 1923 Grouping the line became part of the LNER and with nationalisation became part of the North Eastern Region.

Although there turned out not to be much coal traffic, at one time there was some use of the route to a military gun testing range near Reedsmouth. There was even a whisky train, but livestock, in particular sheep, provided much traffic. Double-headed trains were sometimes required to Bellingham market and Reedsmouth shed could contain up to a dozen engines at busy times.

Passenger services were always rather slow and limited across this sparsely populated area. In 1910 the basic weekday service comprised three passenger trains in each direction. Trains stopped at most stations and took over 100 minutes to travel the 42 miles (68km) between Riccarton and Hexham. The single line also provided part of an alternative route between Newcastle and Edinburgh. This journey usually involved changing trains at Riccarton Junction, or Hawick, and took about six hours. There were some tourists to view the remote scenery, but passenger traffic did not develop and by 1955 a surprisingly similar service to that of 1910 was provided. Three

weekday trains, calling at most stations and taking about 100 minutes, ran in each direction over the Riccarton-Hexham section.

The passenger link from Reedsmouth Junction to Morpeth closed in September 1952. Closure of the remaining limited passenger service was probably inevitable and the last regular passenger train ran between Hexham and Riccarton Junction in October 1956. At Falstone a lament was played on the pipes and lonely goodbyes acknowledged the final passenger services along the route. Through freight remained over the line for a couple more years, but a remaining southern section, from Reedsmouth to Bellingham, was reached via Morpeth and was used by freight trains until November 1963. In addition, an occasional passenger special used this surviving section to serve Bellingham Fair until September 1964.

In 1981 about six miles of the line were lost under the Kielder Reservoir, but a number of other sections of the line are used as public footpaths and the Kielder Viaduct has been preserved. There are even plans to consider reopening the northern section from Kielder to Longtown, on the former Waverley route, for timber freight associated with the extensive Kielder Forest, there is also a short stretch of preserved line at Saughtree.

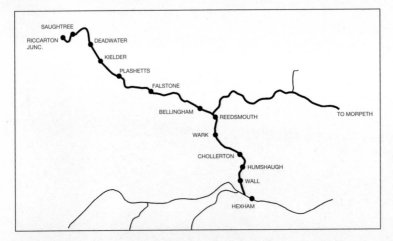

Centre left: Chollerton station with a Hexham-Riccarton Junction train headed by the well turned out Gresley 2-6-2T No 67639 on a misty day in the 1950s. *A. Wickens*

Bottom left: The remote Reedsmouth Junction station with signalbox and water tower. After closure and a period of dereliction the water tower was converted into an attractive house, although the signalbox became the target of much vandalism. This view looking north was taken in September 1971. *N. Stead*

Above right: 'Hunt' Class D49 4-4-0 No 62771 *The Rufford* pauses at Reedsmouth with the 4.27pm Newcastle-Hawick train on 9 June 1956. Reedsmouth engine shed can be seen in the background; after closure of the line it was turned into a farm store. *I. S. Carr*

Below right: Shunting at Bellingham station with ex-NER Class J27 0-6-0 No 65819 prior to complete closure in the early 1960s. In addition to domestic coal, Bellingham market could produce considerable livestock freight. *W. Smith*

Above left: Ex-NER Class J21 No 65110 heads a Riccarton Junction-Hexham train at Bellingham on 20 September 1952. Note the spindly electric lamp post, one of the few items of later investment in this route. *J. W. Armstrong*

Left: The rather austere stone Bellingham station exterior, looking on to the former platform in April 1973. Note the wooden window shutters and the station clock. After closure the station area was used as a council depot. *A. Muckley*

Above: A Derby Lightweight DMU with the annual excursion to the Bellingham Show reverses off the Morpeth line onto the remaining stub of the Riccarton line which ran as far as Bellingham. The excursion train was worked via the Wansbeck Valley branch from Morpeth, and is seen here at Reedsmouth Junction on 22 September 1962. The last such excursion ran in 1964. *M. C. Reed*

Centre right: The remote Plashetts station with its substantial water tower, looking towards Reedsmouth Junction. After closure part of the trackbed here was used as a road during the construction of the Kielder reservoir. The station buildings were later demolished and now lie submerged beneath Kielder Water. *N. Stead*

Right: The castellated stone viaduct south of Kielder dates from 1862 and is seen here in September 1971. A plaque states that the viaduct is the finest surviving example of the skew arch form of construction. The viaduct crosses Kielder Burn and has been preserved as an Ancient Monument. *A. Muckley*

Left: The isolated Kielder Forest station. Noted in the *abc Guide* as 323 miles from King's Cross, in 1956 the 3rd class return fare to London was £5 1s 4d (c£5.06p). The station was located in what was to become the largest man-made forest in Europe. *Ian Allan Library*

Below: Deadwater station, the last on the line in England, looking towards Reedsmouth in February 1981. The limit of the North Eastern Region's territory extended across the Scottish border to the next station at Saughtree. *A. Muckley*

23 A present of the past

Railways started a revolution greater than any other. From modest public passenger beginnings in the northeast, railways developed to provide the safest and most civilised form of transport ever conceived. They went on to change the world, creating and breaking whole empires and stretching to the furthest parts of the map.

The increase in competition in the 1920s, together with the growing recession, saw finances falter. In the northeast the Allendale-Hexham, Alnwick-Coldstream, Amble-Chevington, Cawood-Selby and Lofthouse-in-Nidderdale to Pateley Bridge passenger services all ceased in 1930. Just as the northeast had led the world in the development of railways, it was also prominent in their decline. Sadly, railways went into a period of general retreat. As a consequence, lost lines can be found throughout the world. Indeed, it is estimated that at least 100,000 miles of track have been closed in the USA alone since the 1930s.

In the northeast, decline and closure eventually resulted in a new wealth of lost lines and disused railway structures. The area is proud of its railway past, which is increasingly recognised as an opportunity for the present. Darlington North Road station operates both as a museum and a station. York goods depot is now part of the NRM. Monkwearmouth station, Soho Engine Shed, Dunstan Staithes and many other former railway buildings and structures have been saved. A network of railway paths has also been created, providing access to the countryside as well as reaching deep into urban areas.

Thankfully the closure programme is now at an end and many lines still remain. In the northeast the ECML has been upgraded and new lines have been built for the Tyne and Wear Metro. Some routes have reopened for freight, such as that to Boulby. A significant number of lines have been preserved and there is an impressive and ever growing list of museums and preservation schemes. These offer an experience of

Below: A Bagnall 0-4-0 storms up to Moor Road on the Middleton Railway. This former mineral system dates back to 1758 and in 1812 used steam traction. The Middleton Railway was the first standard gauge line to be preserved and passenger trains run along part of the old route. *M. Leak*

railways past, with an encounter of present northeastern friendliness.

As road congestion and pollution grow, the greater use of railways and reopening of lost lines becomes an inevitability. The railway renaissance is here, railways are now seen as an essential part of tomorrow's transport needs. Proposals that prejudice the future reuse of lost lines are at last being prevented. The pioneering spirit of George Stephenson would be gratified to know that, as civilisation reaches another millenium, railways will be an increasingly important part of that civilisation.

Above: Ex-NER No 2392 shunts a works train in Oakworth Yard on the Keighley & Worth Valley Railway. In 1967, as 'J27' No 65894, the engine was saved from the breaker's yard. Preserved railways such as this, which provide a glimpse of the past, are presently great tourist attractions in the area. *S. Lindsey*

Left: The northeast has done much to commemorate its railway heritage. Rowley station, near Consett, was reassembled at the North of England Open Air Museum at Beamish where it was joined by ex-NER 0-6-0 No 876 (BR 'J21' No 65033). No 876 is seen passing under the ex-NER footbridge in July 1976. *I. S. Carr*

Above: York goods depot in 1908. The disused railway depot was turned into the Peter Allen Building, a splendid extension to the National Railway Museum. *Courtesy NRM*

Right: The front two cars from an eight-car DMU at Eastgate on 10 September 1983. A number of special trains used this freight line prior to its purchase in 1996 by the Weardale Railway. It is heartening to see yet another line saved in the northeast. *M. Hall*

Left: Loftus station with new track in place when this view was taken in February 1973. A section of line from near Skinningrove reopened for freight as far as Boulby in 1974 after earlier closure of this section of the coastal route to Whitby.
A. Muckley

Above: Many lines remain in the northeast. This view was taken in 1967 at Glaisdale station, on the surviving Esk Valley line to Whitby. Clearly at this time the station had not seen much new investment since it was opened, but it survived the Beeching axe, together with many other stations in the northeast. *Author*

Left: Tempus fugit; a view taken in 1997 from within the huge clock of the former Gare d'Orsay, now the Musée d'Orsay. This vast and elegant Parisian station is used today as an art gallery and is part of a magnificent worldwide railway heritage that can be traced back to a distant past in northeast England. *R. Trill*